Citizenship and Governance
in a Changing City

D0625057

Citizenship and Governance in a Changing City

SOMERVILLE, MA

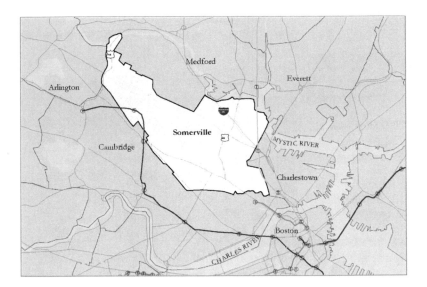

Susan A. Ostrander

TEMPLE UNIVERSITY PRESS   PHILADELPHIA

TEMPLE UNIVERSITY PRESS
Philadelphia, Pennsylvania 19122
www.temple.edu/tempress

Copyright © 2013 by Temple University
All rights reserved
Published 2013

Regional map (page iii): Mapping prepared by the City of Somerville. Courtesy of Mayor Joseph A. Curtatone, Office of Strategic Planning and Community Development, Somerville Transportation Equity Partnership, and the U.S. Census

Library of Congress Cataloging-in-Publication Data

Ostrander, Susan A.
  Citizenship and governance in a changing city : Somerville, MA / Susan A. Ostrander.
      pages cm
  Includes bibliographical references and index.
  ISBN 978-1-4399-1012-2 (cloth : alk. paper) —
ISBN 978-1-4399-1013-9 (pbk. : alk. paper) —
ISBN 978-1-4399-1014-6 (e-book) 1. Community development—Massachusetts—Somerville. 2. Civic improvement—Massachusetts—Somerville. 3. City planning—Massachusetts—Somerville—Citizen participation. 4. Political participation—Massachusetts—Somerville. 5. Citizenship—Massachusetts—Somerville. 6. Somerville (Mass.)—Politics and government. I. Title.
  HN80.S566O88 2013
  307.1'4097444—dc23

                                                    2012041288

♾ The paper used in this publication meets the requirements of the American National Standard for Information Sciences—Permanence of Paper for Printed Library Materials, ANSI Z39.48-1992

Printed in the United States of America

2 4 6 8 9 7 5 3 1

Contents

Acknowledgments

The people who contributed most to identifying and defining the issues in this book are the actively engaged residents of Somerville, Massachusetts, a city with a long and compelling history, where the challenges are great and the collective drive to create a thriving and diverse community is strong and vibrant. In that sense, this study is an example of community-based research. Over more than two decades, students in my sociology classes at Tufts University took part in community learning projects in a variety of Somerville organizations. Gradually, the work they did and the community co-teachers and active residents with whom they worked drew me more and more into the life of the city as both a researcher and a scholar-activist.

In the hope that I have not left someone out, I thank the following people who helped shape my thinking for this book: Nelson Salazar, Alex Pirie, Franklin Dalembert, Warren Goldstein-Gelb, Danny LeBlanc, Lisa Brukilacchio, Jack Connolly, Jim Green, Marty Martinez, Matt McLaughlin, Luis Anthony Morales, Mark Neidergang, Ellin Reisner, Bill Roache, Ben Echevarria, Melissa McWhinney, Tom Bent, Fred Berman, Regina Bertholdo, Walter Pero, Victor DoCouto, Adam Dash, Consuelo Perez, Teresa Cardoso, and Patricia Montes. My academic colleagues and my writing group helped me to frame the concerns of Somerville residents in relation to larger conceptual questions about civic and political engagement and shared governance and what scholars in the field are calling "social citizenship." Thanks go especially to Sarah Sobieraj, Paula Aymer, Frinde Maher, Laura Miller,

Peter Levine, Jeff Berry, Carmen Sirianni, Anna Sandoval, Chris Bobel, Julie Nelson, and Ryan Centner. Also useful were conversations with several faculty and staff members involved in the work of Tufts University's Tisch College of Citizenship and Public Service, as well as the monthly meetings of the Civic Engagement Research Group, which culminated in my 2007 co-edited volume with Kent Portney, *Acting Civically: From Urban Neighborhoods to Higher Education* (New England University Press/Tufts University Press, 2007). Papers that I presented at the annual meetings of the Association for Research on Nonprofit Organizations and Voluntary Action (ARNOVA) in 2009, 2010, and 2011 and the Urban Affairs Association in 2009 provided opportunities for critical commentary from fellow panelists and audience members. Swapna Maruri, my undergraduate research assistant, made substantial contributions to the research. John LiBassi, my department's staff assistant, got the final manuscript into shape for submission to the publisher during a busy week in the semester. I am grateful to them.

Like most research projects, this one is rooted in an aspect of my personal story—in this case, linked to my abiding interest in socioeconomic and other inequalities. Ultimately, then, I must also thank all those people (whom I will refrain from attempting to name) who have played pivotal roles over my three decades of writing and teaching and acting around those issues. I told my own class story in an essay published in a 2003 edited volume called *Our Studies, Ourselves: Sociologists' Lives and Work* (Oxford University Press, 2003). Readers familiar with my first book, *Women of the Upper Class* (Temple University Press, 1984), and my second, *Money for Change: Social Movement Philanthropy at Haymarket People's Fund* (Temple University Press, 1995), may not see the connections between those books and this study. For me the link is clear: What I always want to understand is how people on the inside establish and hold on to power and how those outside challenge and struggle and sometimes are able to reorganize power. The women from old-wealth backgrounds whom I interviewed for my 1984 book had every intention of holding fast to their privileged class position, even if it meant losing ground in gender terms. In vivid contrast, wealthy donors at the Haymarket Fund acted to counter, even demolish, their own class position as they gave up their inherited wealth and generated income to support progressive social movement work, with the contention "Giving to others what belongs to you is charity. Giving to others what belongs to them is social justice" (quoted in Ostrander 1995: 62). The research for this current book about Somerville, like the research for the Haymarket book, has made me see that the questions of who holds power and how and why they hold it are complex in yet another way. Those who still hold power in Somerville proudly claim a working-class heritage; they are not elites in class terms. They also proudly herald their own immigrant origins (usually Irish or Italian), even as they may resist efforts by more recent working-class immigrants (often Latino, Brazilian, or Haitian) to gain a meaningful foothold in local governance. As is true in other studies of power and challenges to power, the questions of who takes which "side" and how and under what circumstances are also complex. I thank all the people of Somerville for telling me their story, which continues to unfold. I do not know how many of them will agree with my expression of what they shared with me. I do know that they will keep on inventing and reinventing their community, as they have for a very long time. I wish them well, and I look forward to remaining a small part of their ongoing efforts.

1
Introduction

> Despite our relative peace, we live with a persistent undercurrent of tension—Between those who have lived here all their lives and those who are new; Between those born in this country and those who are recent immigrants; Between those who can afford rising housing costs and those who are just getting by; Between those who seek immediate action on development issues and those who seek a different vision. (Curtatone 2004)

Based on a multiyear qualitative study from 2004 to 2009 of a mid-size city adjacent to Boston, this book explores local influences that facilitate or pose barriers to civic and political engagement in the public life of an urban community. The book shows how civic and political engagement play out in Somerville, where residents are divided by class, race-ethnicity, and immigrant diversity and where local government is in the eyes of many an entrenched political structure.

This book informs current debates about the place of immigrants in civic and political life and the role of voluntary associations in local politics and government. Some argue that host communities should actively facilitate immigrant incorporation because large numbers of "nonparticipating, unrepresented, [and] disengaged" residents weaken local democracy and community solidarity (Andersen 2008: 77; Bloemraad 2006). A contrasting view claims that only immigrants who have achieved full legal citizenship are entitled to be politically engaged. As for voluntary associations, some say these valuable agents of civil society should avoid politics altogether and focus instead on activities that build community cohesion and solidarity.[1] Others argue that voluntary associations are important vehicles for active citizens (and non-citizens) to affect public decisions and for democracy itself to thrive, thus requiring that associational activity connect to politics and government (Foley and Edwards 1997; Mark R. Warren 2001).

At its root, this book is about the practice of local democracy. When people take part in the civic and political life of their own communities, their actions create a strong foundation for democracy. Democracy overall depends, then, on local involvement to build democratic participation from the ground up (Elstub 2008: 181; King 2004; Mark R. Warren 2001: 21). Especially for those who have not previously been engaged, such as new immigrants, local participation is often the starting point for participation at higher levels (Hardy-Fanta 2002: 196; Mark R. Warren 2001: 22).

The central claim of this book is that full community membership, belonging, and acceptance by others—what I call social citizenship—is a key condition for a kind of democratic participation that I term shared governance.[2] Social citizenship is "full membership in the community within which one lives" (Glenn 2011: 3). Citizenship in this broader sociological sense is "not just a matter of formal legal status; it is rather a kind of belonging which requires recognition by other members of the community" and revolves around social relations of exclusion and inclusion (Glenn 2011: 3; see also Bloemraad 2006 and Glenn 2000).[3] Instead of focusing on legal rights of citizenship, my study is, then, concerned with the actual local practice or substance of citizenship as a socially meaningful category (Glenn 2011: 3). In Somerville, as I show, actively engaged residents who were "born and raised" in the city typically have full social citizenship, while Latino,[4] Brazilian, and Haitian "newcomers" do not enjoy this privilege, even when they are legal citizens. This is true, even though, during my study, the mayor of Somerville appealed to what I am calling social citizenship when he regularly and publicly welcomed to his city everybody who "wants to live here, work hard, and make a positive contribution," saying, "I don't care what your [legal] status is" (Dreilinger 2007: 4).

The concept of shared governance refers to a process for making public decisions that involves actors from both inside and outside government in an ongoing and dynamic way.[5] Typical actors are organizations, especially voluntary associations and community nonprofits.[6] Democratic shared governance operates according to "principles of openness, participation, [and] accountability" (Garcia 2006: 745). Civic engagement scholars describe various forms of democratic shared governance, all of which result in socially produced agreements about public issues arrived at by those in positions of elected authority plus non-governmental actors who challenge state actors to adopt different ends or collaborate with them to achieve common ends.[7]

This social production of public decisions is not intended as a substitute for government, nor is it anti-government. It is a sharing of power, a way for elected officials and engaged members of communities to actively negotiate and adapt to one another's positions. I show how voluntary associations involved in public affairs in Somerville have been able to retain their independence from local government while still engaging with local government in ways that constitute shared governance. Associations do this by determining for themselves when to collaborate with government and when to assume a more distinctive and/or adversarial role. Retaining this choice, I argue, alleviates well-founded concerns about the risks voluntary associations take when they work too closely with government and lose their capacity to speak and act outside the realm of state power.

Because inclusivity of all segments of a population is so important for democracy, I am especially interested in local opportunities and conditions for engagement that bring diverse residents together and those that push them apart (Mark R. Warren 2001: 25). People in Somerville talk about three main groups of residents. First are older residents identified as working class, mainly of Irish and Italian heritage, who were "born and raised" in the city and who still run the local politics. At the time of my study, they constituted the largest ethnic-identified ancestry group (Office of Strategic Planning and Community Development [OSPCD], 2009b: 55) (Figure 1.1). Second is a growing professional middle class, largely white and often (but not always) young. Many of them moved from neighboring towns when housing costs there became prohibitive in the 1980s. Third are newer immigrants, mainly from Central and South America, especially Brazil and El Salvador, and from Haiti (OSPCD 2009b). Some moved to Somerville in the 1980s, driven by violence in their home countries (Figure 1.2).

Based on the old white ethnic working-class power structure, both the newer immigrants of color and the white, middle-class groups are considered newcomers, even though many have lived in Somerville since the 1980s. Being a newcomer in this context often simply means not being "born and raised" in the city or not tracing one's family back three or four generations. One way that the two newcomer groups are excluded from full social citizenship is by the members of "old Somerville" defining them as having arrived in the city more recently than is actually the case.

Immigration is, of course, a major issue in the United States today. The editors of a recent encyclopedic volume on U.S. immigration since 1965

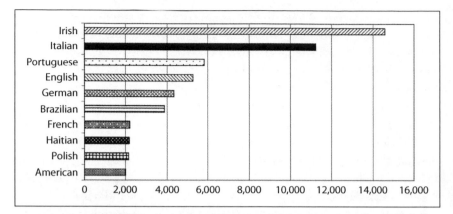

Figure 1.1. Ancestries Most Frequently Reported by Somerville Residents, 2000. *(Office of Strategic Planning and Community Development [OSPCD], Trends in Somerville: Population Technical Report [Somerville, MA: City of Somerville, 2009], 55. Data from the U.S. Census.)*

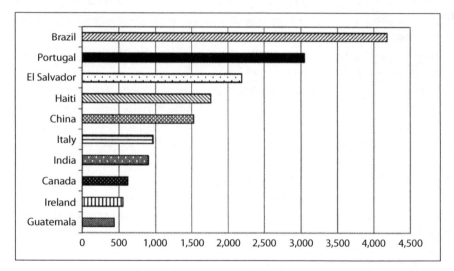

Figure 1.2. Countries of Origin Most Frequently Reported for Foreign-Born Somerville Residents, 2000. *(Office of Strategic Planning and Community Development [OSPCD], Trends in Somerville: Population Technical Report [Somerville, MA: City of Somerville, 2009], 55. Data from the U.S. Census.)*

wrote that "Somerville typifies numerous American neighborhoods where multiplying food stands, restaurants, stores, markets, and mass media vendors have been established by the new American immigrants" (Waters and Ueda 2007: 1). Somerville has experienced substantial growth in Latino and other new immigrant populations since the 1980s. Like other cities, it is dealing with how to adapt to and incorporate these groups into community life. Civic engagement scholars have just begun to explore what it might mean for U.S. democracy if substantial numbers of new immigrants to U.S. towns and cities become more politically engaged (Junn and Haynie 2008: 2). Some research suggests that immigrants today are more engaged than one might expect, even when they are not eligible to vote (Barreto 2003; Marschall 2001). The marches and demonstrations of immigrant groups in the spring of 2006 in the United States brought to light the potential for immigrant engagement (Ramakrishnan and Bloemraad 2008a: 1). As U.S. immigrants become more involved in the public life of their communities, how will local power structures change? How could civic leaders and elected officials assist in the incorporation of immigrants into civic and political life? What local policies might increase the civic and political engagement of immigrants? (Ramakrishnan and Bloemraad 2008a: 32–33).

Unlike many studies of civic and political engagement that focus on individual-level characteristics as explanations for civic engagement, this book emphasizes external conditions and circumstances in the community and local politic that create both opportunities and barriers for engagement. A number of leading scholars have identified individual-level characteristics that facilitate and inhibit engagement, such as education and being socially well connected (social capital).[8] Individual-level analysis seems to imply a deficit model to explain why some communities have low levels of engagement because it assumes that low engagement is caused by problems with residents themselves, such as a lack of political and civic skills, experience, and interests (Levine 2007: xiv). In contrast, a community-level analysis such as this one points to the need for reform in the policies and practices of local institutions if certain segments of the population are not engaged. Higher levels of community engagement not only strengthen democracy but also contribute to higher standards of living and well-functioning local institutions, such as schools and city government (Levine 2007: 28).

While it seems well established that the individual-level factors most associated with high levels of engagement are education and income, this may not be true for diverse populations of immigrants. For immigrants, how politics works to either accommodate or constrain their participation may be a more significant factor (Espiritu 2009: 223; Junn 1999: 1417). Research shows that local responses to immigration in terms of providing these opportunities vary widely. Some local communities in the United States take measures to affirm and protect immigrant residents in ways that encourage incorporation into their communities. Federal government efforts may instead deny and limit the incorporation of immigrants (Wells 2004: 1308).

The positive changes in Somerville that I describe here have been hard won. Beginning in the early 1960s and continuing into the 1980s, this city was known around the region as Slumerville, a decidedly pejorative term despised by today's longtime residents.[9] This widely used local slur brings to mind deteriorating homes, empty storefronts, gritty streets and neighborhoods, and corrupt city administrations associated with organized crime. The 2006 critically acclaimed film *The Departed*—starring Leonardo DiCaprio, Matt Damon, and Jack Nicholson—vividly portrayed Somerville's all too real and horribly violent Winter Hill Gang of those earlier decades (Hassett 2008b).

The changes that have occurred in Somerville happened in large part because of active engagement by Somerville residents, both inside and outside government. From the mid-1960s and continuing to the present, reform-minded residents launched a transformation of what was once a city in decline to one now celebrated for its racial-ethnic and class diversity, thriving arts scene, local festivals, and trendy restaurants and café venues. Somerville is well suited, then, to this study of civic and political engagement. In 1972 and again in 2009, the National Civic League designated it an All America City, which a local newspaper described on the occasion of the 2009 award as a "civic Oscar," celebrating civic engagement, community activism, innovation, and inclusiveness (Federico 2009b).

Local voluntary associations are common vehicles for residents to become involved in local public affairs, not only in Somerville but also elsewhere. Civic engagement scholars define associations as the heart of civil society, providing "a strong community foundation . . . for a vibrant political life" (Mark R. Warren 2001: 15). Associations of greatest interest here are genuine political actors that seek to both influence and participate directly in public decision making (Fung 2003a) through what I call shared governance.

The amount of civic engagement that takes place in Somerville can perhaps be explained in part by two contextual and historical factors: (1) the presence of a city government that, while it has undergone enormous improvement, is still emerging from older patronage practices; and (2) the absence of a strong and vibrant business sector after the decline of an industrial economy. Somerville's city government is also under-resourced because of the loss of its earlier industrial economic base and the more recent loss of revenue from the state of Massachusetts (Hassett 2007c). The lack of a strong local commercial base means that Somerville must rely on resident property taxes for three-quarters of its annual budget. Funding from the state of Massachusetts has been the source of most of the remaining quarter of the budget. As elsewhere in the United States since the national 2008 recession, state budget cuts have resulted in loss of revenue to local cities and towns. These past and current factors have prevented the formation in Somerville of what political scientists characterize as the typical urban regime, made up of powerful combined business and political sectors (Kilburn 2004; Mossberger and Stoker 2001; Stone 1993). This absence opens a space for civic engagement, allowing civil society associations and organizations to obtain greater influence and power in Somerville than might otherwise be the case.

A few caveats: My purpose here differs from research that shows how voluntary associations imbue individuals with knowledge of how to become active citizens by developing civic skills and virtues, increasing their sense of efficacy, or providing political information (Fung 2003a: 518). While political socialization of this kind can indeed encourage participation such as voting, membership in civic and political groups, and attendance at public meetings (Sampson et al. 2005), that is not the focus of this book.

This book also is not intended as an organizational study. It is instead in the tradition of ethnographic studies of entire communities, though focused specifically on characteristics that either facilitate or threaten collective engagement. My interest here, discovered rather than pre-assumed, is local voluntary associations as vehicles for that engagement. Unlike formally constituted community nonprofits, the voluntary associations I studied do not typically keep records of formal membership, so what I was able to learn about numbers and demographics was based on my observations of those who attended meetings. Readers will also note the absence of data on budgets or staff because these associations have neither. I also derived information about why and how these associations were formed and the extent to which they operate according to democratic structures and processes from the kinds of sources used for this study, which I detail in the section on methods.

Finally, this book is by no means a comprehensive look at the city and community of Somerville. Other studies could focus more than this one does on, for example, what is occurring among the city's youth, in schools, religious, cultural, and social service organizations, or on issues of crime, public health, and safety.

Issues of gender might also deserve greater attention, and a gender imbalance in Somerville's elected officials is certainly evident.[10] Feminist scholars have sometimes argued that women tend to focus their civic and political involvement mainly around issues of immediate importance to them, such as families and children as well as women's safety and security (Naples 1998a, 1998b). Because this study centers on the major forms of engagement occurring in the city at the time of my research, concerning redevelopment and immigrant issues, I may have missed some aspects of engagement particular to women. I did note that women were often in positions of leadership in the voluntary associations of greatest interest here and in the more formally constituted community organizations sometimes affiliated with those associations. In the years of my study, both the Somerville Transportation Equity Partnership (STEP) and East Somerville Neighbors for Change (ESNC) were led by women, one white, the other black Haitian. The executive directors of Centro Presente and the Community Action Agency of Somerville were both women (one Latina and one African American). The executive director of the Haitian Coalition was a black Haitian man, although its board of directors was predominantly composed of women. The immigrant advocacy organization called the Welcome Project and the city's community development agency called the Somerville Community Corporation had white men in the top staff positions, but the boards were made up of a majority of women.

In my systematic observations of meetings of various kinds, I saw neither gender differences nor inequalities in how people treated one another, and a search through interview transcripts for references to gender issues or concerns turned up few. My past gender research (Ostrander 1984, 1999, 2004b) suggested that this is somewhat surprising, and I can only speculate that Somerville's enormous changes, whose effect has related primarily to class, race, and immigrant status, may have obscured or overridden more gendered concerns.

Gender issues, however, were not totally absent in interviews. One woman immigrant activist who had founded a women's group spoke about sexual harassment, especially for the women who worked as domestics and were undocumented and therefore afraid to complain. She also noted that immigrant women made less money than the men and reported that some men objected to their wives being employed and said this issue caused conflict and sometimes divorce. Another immigrant woman activist talked about how she had learned her leadership skills while involved in an association well known in the Boston area called One Hundred Black Women, and she spoke about the valued influence of her mother as a "woman full of wisdom and a powerhouse woman." A lifelong female resident of Italian American descent who had risen to be an important leader in the city's business community told about how she had first gone to nursing school, a traditional woman's occupation. When telling me about their family histories, people often spoke with respect and admiration of the struggles their mothers and grandmothers, in particular, had experienced in coming to America and raising children in a foreign culture. The woman who was the first person of Portuguese descent to be elected to public office in Somerville, as a member of the school board, attributed her involvement in education to her mother's inability to be involved at all because she could not speak English. A young man of Irish American heritage who is a youth organizer told of his grandmother, who worked at the local Hostess factory and earned enough to buy the house where he and the rest of his family still live.

Preview of Major Research Findings and Conclusions

At the center of civic and political engagement in Somerville today is public decision making regarding huge redevelopment projects that are fundamentally remaking the city. A critical challenge is how to create a new economic base for this formerly industrial city without displacing its long-standing working class and newer immigrant groups. Somerville residents often discuss this challenge as being about the tension between the benefits and dangers of gentrification, a topic of much interest to urban scholars.

While some Somerville immigrants who are active in their community do concern themselves with redevelopment issues (especially the preservation of affordable housing and the availability of jobs), active engagement by the city's immigrant groups tends toward more immediate local events that threaten immigrant safety and security. As I explain, this is one of the reasons why I argue that members of newer immigrant groups in the city, whether legal citizens or not, do not enjoy full social citizenship. In recent years, one event demanding immigrants' attention was the 2004 adoption of a local gang ordinance that Latino leaders see as marginalizing and stigmatizing Latino youth. Another was the summer 2007 and 2008 federal Immigration and Customs Enforcement (ICE) raids that brought fear to anyone in the city who "looked Latino" and led to a flurry of organizing aimed at protecting immigrants.[11]

I claim here that at the root of active involvement of Somerville residents lies a deeper and larger struggle about who should be the city's elected leaders and how they should conduct the city's affairs. On one side of this struggle are the relative newcomers to the city, both newer immigrants and members of a new non-immigrant middle class, who are trying to gain a foothold in the city's politic. I conceptualize this as an effort to be admitted to full community membership (social citizenship) and participation in shared governance. On the other side is Somerville's political "old guard," which has changed very little since 1929, when Irish working-class immigrants wrested control from the city's Yankee elite founders.

The circumstances and opportunities for Somerville's two newcomer groups to participate in community affairs are, of course, both different and

unequal. The growing professional, largely white middle class includes politically active progressives who have lived in the city since the 1980s, some
forced to move from the contiguous city of Cambridge as housing costs rose
rapidly in that community. Somerville's new middle class also consists of
young professionals who value the city for its proximity to Boston, its relatively lower housing costs, and its hip urban feel. They can be characterized
as devotees of a new urban renaissance culture that sees life in the suburbs as
one of bland homogeneity. Both segments of this growing middle class have
begun to make inroads into elected offices, with one elected to the Board of
Aldermen and several to the School Committee.

The other population making up Somerville's "newcomers" is a relatively
well-established but politically unorganized population of immigrants who
are mainly working-class; mostly Latino, Brazilian, and Haitian; and largely
of color. For them, English is a second or third language. Even though some
of these "new" immigrants have lived in Somerville for two decades or more,
up to the time of my study, they had not gained a single elected position in
the city. Their few attempts to gain elected office have ended in failure, and a
small number of administrative appointments of individuals from this population have been short-lived.

Somerville city government and the city generally are officially welcoming to new immigrants. The city's popular mayor, a second-generation immigrant[12] of Italian heritage, took office in 2004, when he was only thirty-eight
years old. In 2009, he was reelected without opposition for a third two-year
term. He is well known for the creation of new civic spaces for the city's
young urban professionals[13] (referred to as yuppies by old-timers) and for his
public support of immigrants. All of the city's elected leaders with whom I
spoke or whom I heard speak at public meetings or whose quotes I read in
local newspapers regularly expressed pride in Somerville's legacy as an immigrant city. They want new immigrants to continue to come to the city to
live, and they support the rights of immigrants to have equal access to local
jobs, affordable housing, city services, public protection of their safety, and
freedom from ethnic and racial prejudice. To a person, they oppose using
local police to enforce federal laws about illegal immigrants, and they have
no interest in actively pursuing or even identifying an unknown number of
undocumented immigrants who live in their city.

At the same time, when I asked longtime elected officials what the city
might *do* to bring the city's newer immigrants into the polity as full members, their answers focused on the responsibility of new immigrants themselves to "just get involved," with the idea that eventually they would "just
naturally" begin to ascend to elected posts in city government. When local

immigrant leaders and advocates proposed concrete institutional reforms, such as routine language translation at city meetings, regular printing of city documents and public announcements over the city's call system in multiple languages, routine voter registration drives in immigrant neighborhoods, multi-lingual ballots, and extension of the ability to vote in local elections to non-citizens, the response of elected officials, with very few exceptions, ranged from passivity to active resistance.

In 2008 and 2009, for example, Somerville's Board of Aldermen declined to sign on to an immigrant-led initiative, even though the mayor and subsequently the elected School Committee readily endorsed it. That initiative, known as Welcoming Somerville, called for the community to be "hospitable, welcoming and inclusive of diversity" and stated that "harsh immigration enforcement policies violate civil and human rights of immigrants, that workplace and home raids must end immediately and that our nation must implement a humane and just reform of our immigration laws" (website of Massachusetts Immigrant and Refugee Advocacy Coalition, accessed June 11, 2009). I return to this initiative in my discussion of immigrant civic engagement (see Chapter 5).[14] Old-time city officials' lack of support for measures that would open up local politics to the one-third of the population that is made up of newer immigrants reinforces my conclusion that underneath the most visible and active forms of resident civic and political engagement lies a deeper ongoing local power struggle over who and how this city will be governed.

Conceptual Framework and Theoretical Contribution

I began my study with a broad definition of civic engagement as "individual and collective action to identify and address public concerns and to participate in public life" (Ostrander and Portney 2007: 1). This definition suggests that engagement with debates about community issues and concerns, that is, with politics, broadly defined, is necessary for people to exert some control over public matters that affect their lives (Foley and Edwards 1997; Mark R. Warren 2001). I term that measure of control as shared governance. This definition of civic engagement also implies the value of widespread public participation that includes the community's newest members in what I am calling social citizenship.

Driven by what I saw and heard in Somerville, I became especially interested in forms of engagement that go beyond trying to influence local government to exerting real power in making public decisions and becoming at times an integral part of true governing. This idea draws on current understandings of relations between the civic and political realms—between civil society and the state (Choup 2006)—as interactive. It is consistent with notions of democracy that go beyond the state toward a democratic society (Boyte 2005). It draws on emerging frameworks that try to link civil society (where public issues are deliberated, opinions created, and agendas set) to official political realms, where actual decisions about public issues are made (Elstub 2008; Hendriks 2006).

Here is where the concept of mutual or shared governance assumes special importance. As I have said, while conventional views of governance are limited to actions by government (Chaskin 2003: 162), broader notions of governance see public decision making as an outcome of dynamic and ongoing engagement by multiple involved actors, both inside and outside government. Flowing broadly from Foucault's concept of governmentality, civic actors are then seen in relation to multiple sites of governing beyond the traditional boundaries of the state (McKee 2009: 469).

As I show, actions by civic associations in Somerville are, at times, able to at least approach genuine mutual or shared governance. I also demonstrate that this level of participation is much less available to newer immigrant groups because they are not fully accepted and participating members of the community—that is, they lack social citizenship. This is sometimes true even of those who do hold legal citizenship. The point is starkly made by what my research shows about the occasions when Somerville's newer immigrant groups are most likely to become engaged—occasions most often limited to local events that immediately threaten immigrant safety and security, such as raids by federal ICE agents or local actions that are racist and anti-immigrant.

Somerville's civic actors sometimes choose to preserve their independence from local government and avoid cooptation by strategically shifting between being collaborative and adversarial in relation to local government. This avoids their having to depend on the invitation of local government to participate in public decision making.[15] Several conditions in Somerville support civic actors' capacity to function relatively autonomously from city government. As noted earlier, the relative absence of a typical urban regime in Somerville, dominated by business and governmental sectors, creates the potential for genuine political power by voluntary associations and community organizations. While this city's earlier model of political patronage has not completely disappeared, the loss of revenue in recent decades, due in large part to the city's declining economic base, has weakened both governmental and business sectors. Because city government is not well resourced, it cannot wield the kind of power it might otherwise, and that cir-

cumstance increases the potential for influence (and real power) of civil
society groups.

Collaboration with local government around public decision making is
facilitated in Somerville by a relatively harmonious fit between what civically
engaged residents want to achieve and what the city administration wants
to achieve in terms of community and economic development. I discuss this
later by, for example, showing the commonality between two community
visions developed, on one hand, by a process sponsored by the city administration and, on the other, by a parallel but separate process run by a coalition of civic organizations.

The possibility for mutual or shared governance is further strengthened
by a shared allegiance to the Democratic Party. I later describe a bitter relationship between the city's more traditional blue-collar, working-class,
"lunch bucket" Democrats and the newer, largely middle-class Progressive
Democrats of Somerville known as PDSers. Members of both groups acknowledge that their conflict is more a concern about process and style than
a substantive disagreement about issues. I see their conflict as reflecting a
fundamental struggle in the city about who does and does not deserve full
community membership (social citizenship) and who, therefore, will have
the most opportunities to take part in public affairs (shared governance).
One source of conflict is the support of the Progressive Democrats of Somerville for candidates who represent newer immigrants and the newer middle
class and for affirmative measures that would make it easier for newer immigrants to be politically engaged. Traditional Somerville Democrats are opposed to both, perhaps not surprisingly, because these actions threaten their
established position in the city politic.

This larger struggle about who the city's elected leaders will be and how
they will govern is a major area where politically engaged civic associations
sometimes take an adversarial stance toward Somerville's political establishment. The outcome of this struggle is centrally important to this city's
capacity to extend local democracy and to incorporate into its public life
newer residents who are immigrants of color (often low-income and/or working-class people), and a new, relatively privileged, often young and white professional middle class.

Research Methods

This book is based on interviews with forty-five actively engaged Somerville
residents; extensive review of city documents, local and regional newspaper
articles, and city and community websites; plus attendance at some thirty

community and city meetings. The locally engaged residents interviewed for this study were involved in various aspects of local public life: voluntary associations, community nonprofit organizations, business, the arts, elected city government, and church and neighborhood groups. Although I include some elected officials and paid staff of prominent community organizations who also resided in and were active in Somerville, I focus primarily on residents who were involved in their community in a voluntary capacity rather than as paid staff of community organizations or of the city administration. Interviews were conducted between March 2007 and June 2009.

My study's emphasis on the five years between 2004 and 2009 reflects the first five years of the current reform mayor's term in office, during which time he was reelected twice. (As of January 2012, this same mayor began his fifth term in office.) It is always difficult for social scientists doing qualitative field studies like this one to determine when to end data collection and leave the field. This book is, then, like all such studies, inevitably a snapshot in time. In an effort to provide some sense of historical context, I make use of a locally published city history going back to Somerville's earliest years (Haskell n.d.) and one focused on the 1960s and 1970s (Johnston 2009; see also the scholarly studies of Somerville by Levenstein [1976] and Ueda [1987]). I also obtained background information from an online search of local newspapers dating back to 1997.

I left the field in December 2009, at the point when a coalition of community groups and the city administration had completed separate parallel processes that created a set of principles to guide the city for the next twenty years (2010 to 2030). These vision statements, reproduced in Chapter 3, provide a map for civic and political engagement over the next decade. While the story told here ends at that point, the story of the organizations and the people I studied, of course, continues to unfold.[16]

I selected people to interview by perusing lists of involved individuals on city and organization websites, noting individuals and groups that received multiple mentions in the local newspapers, and making contacts when I attended meetings. I also asked interview subjects to provide additional names, and I interviewed only people who were independently suggested by at least two others. Although I do not live in Somerville, I am a longtime engaged faculty member at Tufts University, which is located partially in Somerville. My more than two decades of practice placing students in Somerville agencies gave me the access I needed and the opportunity to become familiar with the city and to become known and trusted by key local actors (Ostrander 2004a; Ostrander and Portney 2007).

People who were interviewed were chosen in roughly equal numbers from the different main segments of Somerville's population: ten lifelong residents of Irish and/or Italian heritage; fourteen relative newcomers who were white Anglo and members of the professional middle class; and thirteen members of the city's largest newer immigrant groups of color, namely Latinos of varying nationalities, Brazilians, and Haitians. Eight people of Portuguese or Greek origin were also interviewed. They provide an interesting contrast to the earlier Irish and Italian immigrants who took over the city's political establishment, plus a different and earlier view of the race-based hostility later faced by Latinos, Brazilians, and Haitians.

Interview subjects ranged from twenty-five to seventy-six years of age, with fifty-three years of age the median. Eighteen were women and twenty-seven were men. Confidentiality limits a more detailed description of interview subjects, although they are more fully described as they are quoted throughout this book. Pseudonyms match subjects' ethnic background. Interviews dealt with personal and family history; class, race, and ethnic meaning and identification; and education and job history. Most importantly, I asked about Somerville's social and political divisions and conflicts (and lack thereof), impressions of the city's political leadership, types of civic and political involvement, and visions of the future of the city. Interviews were sixty to ninety minutes long and took place in subjects' homes or offices. Each interview was audiotaped and transcribed verbatim.

City reports, documents, and materials are readily available and are posted on the city's active and extensive website. Because Somerville is in a period of intense redevelopment, city reports are frequent and voluminous, including detailed city plans required as a condition of funding from federal Community Development Block Grants through the U.S. Department of Housing and Urban Development (HUD) program for lower-income areas of the city. The city plan for the years 2008 to 2013 is some five hundred pages long (OSPCD 2008). I also regularly read two Somerville weekly newspapers considered locally as representing different political points of view, and I monitored websites of key community organizations and associations engaged in city issues. To supplement the interviews and review of written and published materials, I periodically attended meetings of various community nonprofit organizations and voluntary associations, including neighborhood associations, in addition to meetings sponsored by the mayor's office and city department, such as the Human Rights Commission and the Office of Strategic Planning and Community Development.

I analyzed all data—interview transcripts, documents and publications of various kinds, and field notes—using standard qualitative research practices, which aim for the inductive emergence of new ways of thinking (theory broadly defined). The first step is to create analytic categories that arise from the data. This contrasts with research where these categories are deduced post hoc from pre-existing theory. The next step is to use these emergent categories to systematically code all materials. Finally, I searched for relationships among categories as the basis for developing arguments informed by current theoretical knowledge and debates. The literature on this kind of methodology is well established (Berg 2009; Denzin and Lincoln 2000; Esterberg 2002; Lofland and Lofland 1995).

Because this research is an in-depth qualitative study of the civic and political engagement and power politics of a single city, it contains both the strengths and weaknesses of a study that was not based on random samples of a population and was not intended to test hypotheses derived from existing theory. An important value of this kind of study is to provide rich close-to-the-ground qualitative data capable of inductively generating new thinking on a particular topic. Future research may assess that new thinking and its validity in other settings and under other conditions.

I have been somewhat involved in Somerville outside my role as a researcher, a practice that is not uncommon among ethnographic and qualitative researchers. I have for many years arranged for students at my university to do volunteer projects in Somerville community organizations. In the spring semester of 2007, students from one of my classes plus a class taught by a colleague conducted fourteen of the forty-five interviews used in this book. In 2008, I joined the board of directors of a Somerville immigrant advocacy organization called the Welcome Project, which I discuss in later chapters. My invitation to join that board and my acceptance of the offer demonstrate my sympathy toward the concerns and interests of the city's newer immigrants before and during my research.

Plan of the Book

Chapter 2 describes the city that is the subject of this book. The chapter offers a brief economic and political history, introduces its people in all of their diversity, and highlights the fundamental changes that Somerville is experiencing.

Chapter 3 tells the stories of how civic associations of various kinds—advocacy groups, neighborhood associations, and satellite groups affiliated with the city's community development corporation—act and how they have both influenced and become an integral part of public decision making. I show how associations that were not listened to by earlier city administrations turned to an oppositional strategy, bringing several successful legal suits against city government for failing to include community input. The chapter explains how, as the city's reform-oriented young mayor came into office in 2004, active associations, along with city officials, chose more collaborative ways to achieve their goals, while retaining the option of a more adversarial relationship when needed.

Chapter 4 describes immigrant experiences in old and new Somerville as the actively engaged city residents I interviewed described them to me. I talked with first-generation Latino, Brazilian, and Haitian immigrants; first- and second-generation Greeks and Portuguese; and second-, third-, and fourth-generation Irish and Italians. A key focus of these interviews was the similarities and differences between different generations and racial-ethnic groups. The main points include the importance to actively engaged residents of Somerville's tradition as a city where immigrants are welcome and can make a better life for themselves and their families. Common themes are learning English and becoming American citizens. Defying stereotypes of white working-class ethnics as insensitive to matters of race, the actively engaged older white Irish and Italian immigrants I talked with seemed to recognize (often without my asking) that newer immigrants of color face barriers that white immigrants of earlier generations did not.

Chapter 5 is about immigrant civic and political engagement in Somerville, focusing on the newer Latino, Brazilian, and Haitian immigrants and their local allies and advocates. This chapter shows how these newer immigrants actively respond when events threaten them directly. It suggests that an essential condition for immigrant engagement is a local community that offers some measure of protection so that newer immigrants feel relatively safe to act collectively, even at a minimal level. The chapter suggests, as did the people I talked with, ways that local government might act affirmatively to remove barriers to full incorporation into the public life of the community (i.e., barriers to social citizenship that then become barriers to participation in shared governance and local democracy).

Chapter 6 examines what the people I interviewed had to say about the future of their city. Residents told me about the advantages and disadvantages of gentrification, and they offered differing views about their willingness to incorporate both non-immigrant middle-class and immigrant newcomers into the life of the city. This chapter discusses how Somerville residents came together despite their differences to express a common vision for their city. Here I give voice to expressions of appreciation for Somerville's diversity, pride in its working-class and immigrant heritage, and excitement (along with worry) about improvements coming to the city in the next decade. Here in this common vision lies the possibility for Somerville to become a city where all residents can become full members of the community in an extension of social citizenship.

In Chapter 7, class, race, and immigration rise to the center of my analysis as I explore what seems to be the city's most bitter division: the struggle over who occupies elected positions in city government and how they are going to govern. Where Chapter 6 is about coming together, Chapter 7 is about coming apart and the possibility of remaking a city government and democratic process that today is not representative of the population of this changing city. I argue that the deeper struggle that underlies much of the civic and political engagement in the city is about how to extend or withhold the full membership of two very different groups of relative newcomers to Somerville: a community of immigrants, mostly from Central and South America and Haiti, some of whom who have lived in the city for two decades, and a growing number of middle-class, mostly white professionals. Some of the members of this new middle class are decades-long residents, and others are young families or young singles recently graduated from college. It is this struggle that will define who is and who is not able to obtain full social citizenship, with its accompanying opportunity to participate in local shared governance. Here rests the future of politics and power and the state of democracy in the public life of this rapidly changing city.

2

Overview of History, Demographics, and Politics

Thumbnail History, Population Growth, and Decline

Somerville was settled originally in 1630 as part of Boston's Charlestown. The Massachusetts state legislature set Somerville aside as a separate town in 1842, and it formally incorporated as its own city in 1872 (Haskell n.d.; Ueda 1987).[1] Somerville reportedly had to thwart annexation by its neighbors to claim its own charter (Haskell n.d.), and locals today like to claim this history as seeding the tenacious fighting spirit still present in the city's character (Agarwal 2004). More than one person I talked with described local politics with pride and humor as "a blood sport."

Somerville, then, traces its history back nearly four hundred years. In 1630, the first non–Native American resident, John Woolrich, moved from Boston's Charlestown to become neighbor to American Indians who had settled long before in the territory later known as Somerville (Haskell n.d.). In 1631, John Winthrop, the first governor of the Commonwealth of Massachusetts, obtained from the Commonwealth a grant of six hundred acres of land to establish his Ten Hills Farm in the Somerville neighborhood still known as Ten Hills, bordering the Mystic River (Haskell n.d.).

Somerville contains a number of historic Revolutionary War sites, including the place where Paul Revere passed through the city during his famous ride in 1775, warning of the coming of British soldiers, and the place where a skirmish took place that same day in Union Square (which still goes by that name, and which, as I discuss in Chapter 3, is one of the sites currently undergoing major redevelopment). During the decades after the Revolutionary War, the city began to take shape, changing from a solely rural and pastoral area. Boston's prominent Yankee families, known as Boston Brahmins, moved to Somerville from Beacon Hill, initially to escape the summer heat and later to distance themselves from the influx of Irish immigrants who later came to Somerville. The Brahmins built large summer houses in the city, many of which still stand, although few are the single-family dwellings that were built originally.

The first Somerville town meeting took place on April 4, 1842. A high school was erected in 1851. Horses, cars, and street lamps went into service in 1858 and 1859. Sewers were built in 1867. A police court was established in 1872, and a public library opened in 1873 (Haskell n.d.).

In three short decades between 1842 and 1870, the city's population multiplied from one thousand souls to fifteen thousand (Ueda 1987: 8). The 1850s began a time of new ethnic and class tensions as Boston's Irish immigrants began to move to Somerville, then still part of the enclave neighborhood Charlestown. Between 1850 and 1860, immigrants from Ireland grew to one-fifth of the city's population (Ueda 1987: 8, 9), the same proportion of residents with Irish origins today. From 1860 to 1870, "the fields and brickyards of Somerville gradually gave way to looming factory buildings and belching smokestacks. The rush of settlement forced the town's population upward at dizzying speed from 8,025 in 1860 to 14,685 in 1870" (Ueda 1987: 8).

By 1870, just around the time Somerville was declaring itself an independent entity from Charlestown, "the social structure was being polarized into a property-owning business class and a property-less working class. . . . At the top of the social ladder were Yankee businessmen. . . . At the bottom were the immigrant Irish" (Ueda 1987: 13). The Irish entered the very bottom of the social and economic hierarchy, where "meager wages made [them] dependent on [their] children's employment" (Ueda 1987: 47). The volume and array of employment opportunities drew workers to Somerville during this time (Office of Strategic Planning and Community Development [henceforth OSPCD] 2009b: viii). Irish men worked in the city's brickyards, railroad yards, and bleacheries, with their sons alongside them, while mothers and daughters (like Irish immigrant women everywhere in the United States) hired out to the city's Yankee elite families as housekeepers and caretakers of children, the sick, and the elderly. Irish working-class wives and mothers, as they did elsewhere, also took in boarders to make ends meet. Tensions were high at times between Irish Catholic "papists" and Somerville's Protestant upper and working classes, and violence was not unknown.

From 1870 to 1900, Somerville grew rapidly again, from 15,000 to 60,000, four-fold in three decades (Ueda 1987: 83). This was the city's greatest period of population growth (OSPCD 2009b: vii). During this time, the city's main civic buildings were built: the Somerville city hall, the library, and the high school, all occupying the same plot of land. All three of these buildings, little changed in outside appearance, are still in use. By 1900, Somerville was also home to eight passenger railway stations that facilitated migration into the city from other local areas and provided the city's connection to regional job markets (OSPCD 2009b: vii).

Somerville's second-generation Irish began to climb both socially and geographically, moving up the hill from neighborhoods that locals still refer to as the Patch and Brickbottom (the latter named for its industrial brickyards). An Irish middle class consolidated (Ueda 1987: 68), and in the early twentieth century, the city's politics shifted from "Yankee Republican . . . to immigrant Democratic." In 1929, Irishman John Murphy was elected the first Democratic mayor, marking the end of the reign of the city's "ruling elite of Yankee businessmen" (Ueda 1987: 61; Levenstein 1976: 37).

Somerville's evolution from a spacious rural pastoral summer playground for affluent urbanites to a densely populated, working-class industrial immigrant city made possible the election of Mayor Murphy and the first-ever city Board of Aldermen controlled by the Democratic Party. By the beginning of the new century, "Yankee Republicans retreated before the floodtide of immigrants and workers" (Ueda 1987: 186), and by 1920, the majority of Somerville residents had been born somewhere outside the United States (Ueda 1987: 190). Residents today still proudly lay claim to Somerville's heritage as an immigrant city. As Sam Martin, thirty-year resident and prominent immigrant advocate, told me, "It's been a gateway city for a long time, better than a hundred years." I discuss this further in the context of immigrant experiences (see Chapter 4).

By 1930, Somerville was home to nearly 30,000 foreign-born residents with the majority of new immigrants at this time from French Canada, Ireland (still), Italy, and Portugal. Italians were replacing the Irish workers in the packing plants and factories and warehouses as the Irish moved up (Ueda 1987: 189). Later came the Portuguese and Greeks. All were drawn by low-skilled jobs in a thriving industrial economy, homes they could afford, and a rapid public transportation system (Ueda 1978: 186).

Population growth was astonishing, and by 1930 had reached its historic peak, when the U.S. Census reported 103,908 residents, about 25,000 on each of the city's four square miles. Not surprisingly, class and ethnic tensions grew (Ueda 1987: 187, 193). That year, Somerville became the most densely populated city in New England as well as one of the most densely populated in the nation, a distinction it still holds. To accommodate this growing population and to allow multi-generational families to live together, at the turn of the century, working-class families began to build the characteristic triple-decker houses that still dominate Somerville's neighborhoods.

Increasing debate about the quality of life in the city accompanied this period of growing population density and rapid growth and construction. Reformers lamented the loss of open and green space, even, as is true today, they recognized the need for affordable multi-unit housing. Reflecting national trends toward regulation of land use, the city enacted its first zoning ordinance in 1925. This new regulation likely contributed to a slowing of residential construction because only about 20 percent of today's housing stock in the city was built after 1920 (OSPCD 2009b: viii).

After 1930, in the midst of the Great Depression, Somerville's urban industrial economy slid rapidly downward, as it did in similar cities, and new immigration trailed off as the number of jobs decreased (Levenstein 1976: 37). Railroad yards and meat packing companies experienced "long shutdowns and lay-offs" (Levenstein 1976: 36). Automation contributed to the loss of the city's industrial base, and Somerville began a decades-long period of overall decline.

Population decreases continued during the 1950s (OSPCD 2009b: 1). Those who could afford to move out did. This was a time of exodus, aided after World War II by the G.I. Bill home loans, and consistent with the national trend of movement to the suburbs (Levenstein 1976: 132). Many of those able to flee the city were the children and grandchildren of the original Irish and Italians who were moving not only out but also up. For those left behind, property values in Somerville stagnated at the same time as they were rising in surrounding towns. Residents with the least resources were left behind, trapped inside the city limits as jobs disappeared. People were forced to travel daily outside Somerville to find work. Despite relatively high property taxes, the city's coffers depleted as the city spent its resources to help those whose incomes were decreasing or nonexistent (Levenstein 1976: 32, 36). By the early 1980s, as sixty-year-old lifetime resident Sean Russo, who is of Irish and Italian heritage, described it to me: "All of my friends had moved out, maybe two of us left in the city. . . . They moved to Tewksbury, Billerica, West Medford. . . . If I sent you to Tewksbury to interview them, and you asked where they were from, they'd say Somerville."

Humiliating taunts about Slumerville began in the 1960s and 1970s and continued into the next two decades. These still echo painfully for longtime residents. Also during this period, huge highway projects were constructed in a Somerville desperate for revenue (OSPCD 2009b: ix). In 1950, what had been the old Irish neighborhood of Brickbottom was razed to prepare for the Inner Belt Expressway (which was never actually built). That same year, homes in the East Somerville neighborhood called the States were demolished to make way for Interstate 93, a multi-lane highway that still isolates East Somerville from the rest of the city and contributes to the racial-ethnic and class segregation of that neighborhood.

By 1980, Somerville's population had reached its year 2000 level of about 77,000 at the time (OSPCD 2009b: 1). Today Somerville is in a period of major transformation, with ambitious community redevelopment projects aimed at revitalizing the city's economic base. The largest of these projects is Assembly Square, the 145-acre former site of a huge Ford plant that opened in 1928 and closed in 1958. Since the 1970s, the land where the plant once stood has been occupied by a deteriorating shopping mall. I discuss this project and the resident civic engagement around it in some detail in Chapter 3.

Demographic Profile of Somerville Residents in Recent Decades and Today: Race, Ethnicity, Nationality, Language, and Immigrant Status

Somerville's foreign-born population doubled as a percentage of the total population between 1970 and 2000 (OSPCD 2009b: 1). The one-third (30 percent) of Somerville residents who are foreign born are relatively recent arrivals, with three-quarters coming to the United States after 1980 and one-third after 1995 (OSPCD 2009b: 54).

Immigrants from Brazil, El Salvador, and Haiti began coming to Somerville in large numbers during the 1980s when at least ten thousand new immigrants came to the city. In 1993, Boston area's major newspaper declared that "few cities in Massachusetts have been affected as greatly by immigration as Somerville" (Bennett 1993). Today nearly one-half of students in the Somerville public schools grew up speaking a language other than English (Dreilinger 2007).

During the 1990s, the wave of new immigrants rapidly changed the face of the city (Parker 2005b). In just one year, from 1999 to 2000, for example, Somerville's immigrant population increased by 33 percent, from 16,975 to 22,727. In that one year, this city of 77,469 added more than 7,100 Brazilian and Portuguese, 2,188 Salvadorans, 1,765 Haitians, and about 1,100 Chinese (Parker 2005b). By 2003, the director of Somerville's main Haitian community organization estimated that 6,000 Haitians lived there, one-half of them U.S. citizens (Samburg 2003).

The 2000 U.S. Census reported that over three-quarters of Somerville residents (77 percent) were white, and nearly that many (73 percent) were white and non-Hispanic. (During the years of my study, both city officials and community organizations actively engaged in city affairs used the 2000 U.S. Census figures, so that is why I usually do so here.) Nearly one-half of those who were foreign born came from Latin America (45.2 percent), between one-fourth and one-third (29 percent) came from somewhere in Europe, and one-fifth (19 percent) come from Asia (U.S. Census Bureau 2000b).

Reflective of the Irish and Italian heritage "old guard" that still runs the city, fully one in three of today's residents traces origin to these first immigrant groups, either Ireland (19 percent) or Italy (15 percent). One in seven (12 percent) of Somerville residents are Hispanic (U.S. Census Bureau 2005). Unlike other cities in the United States with large Hispanic or Latino populations, nearly all Latino residents of Somerville are from countries other than Mexico, Cuba, or Puerto Rico. Fewer than one-tenth of Somerville residents are black (mostly Haitian), with a few African Americans. The number of blacks increased from 6.5 percent in 2000 to 8.4 percent in 2005. Asians of various ethnic and national origins constituted 6.4 percent of the 2000 population (2005 data not available).

In the nearly two decades between 1990 and 2007, the number of non-citizens in the city grew by about one-third, from 10,798 in 1990, to 15,650 in 2000, to 13,235 in 2007 (U.S. Census Bureau 1990, 2000a, 2007). Local immigrant advocates told me they doubted these figures because that portion of non-citizens who are undocumented are less likely than other residents to respond to requests for information from the U.S. Census Bureau. A 2008 city report estimated that one in five of all Somerville residents are non-citizens, and most of them are here legally (Office of the Mayor 2008: 52). According to the Pew Hispanic Center, 14 percent of Massachusetts residents are immigrants (about 912,310 people), and of these, about 20 percent (about 190,000) are undocumented (Aizenman 2009). Using this 20 percent figure suggests that just over 5,000 undocumented immigrants lived in Somerville during the period of my research, or fewer than one-third of its non-citizens.[2]

U.S. Census data report that the Portuguese-speaking population of Somerville grew from approximately 1,500 in the year 2000 to over 5,000 in 2005, with a few hundred more added by the year 2007.[3] It is highly probable that the large and rapid increase was the result of a large number of Brazilians who came to the city during that time. At the time of the 2000 U.S. Census, Brazilians represented the largest number of foreign-born residents

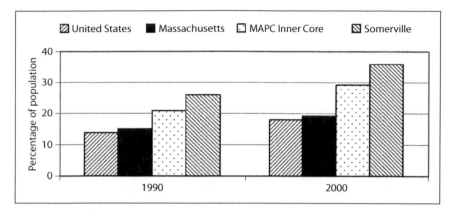

Figure 2.1. Population Speaking a Foreign Language at Home, 1990–2000. MAPC, Metropolitan Area Planning Commission. *(Office of Strategic Planning and Community Development [OSPCD], Trends in Somerville: Population Technical Report [Somerville, MA: City of Somerville, 2009], 56. Data from the U.S. Census.)*

in the city—4,182 in the year 2000, compared with 3,039 Portuguese, 2,188 Salvadorans, 1,765 Haitians, and 1,529 Chinese in the same year (OSPCD 2009b: 55).

About one-third of all Somerville residents (36 percent) speak a language other than English at home (U.S. Census Bureau 2000b), and one-fifth report that they speak English "less than very well," suggesting greater comfort speaking another language (Office of the Mayor 2008: 52) (Figures 2.1 and 2.2). The most common languages are Portuguese (8,932 residents), Spanish (5,794), Haitian Creole (2,023), Italian (1,786), and Chinese (1,639) (OSPCD 2009b: 56).

While newer immigrant groups are dispersed throughout the city, East Somerville has twice as many Hispanics (to use the U.S. Census term) than live in the city as a whole (20 percent versus 9 percent). The eastern part of Somerville has more people of color than any other neighborhood compared with the city as whole (34 percent versus 23 percent). East Somerville is cut off from the rest of the city by a four-lane highway that the city agreed to during the Slumerville period to gain some much-needed revenue. The concentration of Latinos and people of color in this part of the city results in class segregation as well as segregation by race and ethnicity.[4] As many first-generation, low-income immigrants (often of color) have moved to the eastern part of the city in recent decades, young middle- and upper-income professionals (largely white) have moved into the western part of the city (Office of the Mayor 2008: 5) (Figures 2.3 and 2.4).

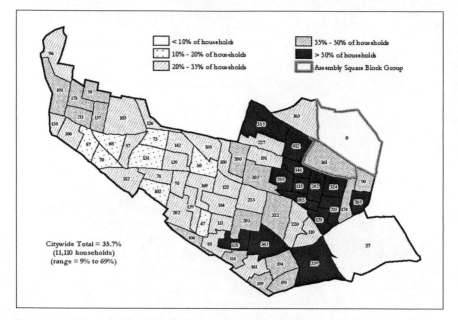

Figure 2.2. Households Primarily Speaking a Foreign Language at Home, 2000. *(Office of Strategic Planning and Community Development [OSPCD],* Trends in Somerville: Population Technical Report *[Somerville, MA: City of Somerville, 2009], 58. Data from the U.S. Census.)*

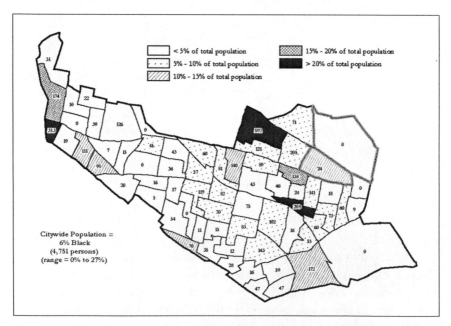

Figure 2.3. Black Population, 2000. *(Office of Strategic Planning and Community Development [OSPCD],* Trends in Somerville: Population Technical Report *[Somerville, MA: City of Somerville, 2009], 50. Data from the U.S. Census.)*

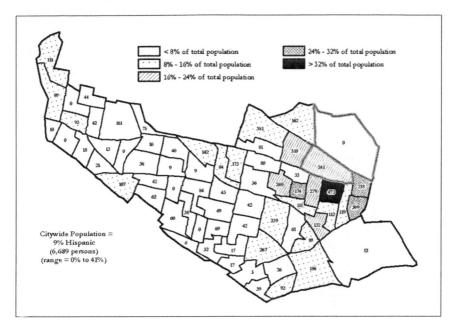

Figure 2.4. Hispanic Population, 2000. *(Office of Strategic Planning and Community Development [OSPCD],* Trends in Somerville: Population Technical Report *[Somerville, MA: City of Somerville, 2009], 51. Data from the U.S. Census.)*

One reason why newer immigrants move into the eastern part of Somerville is that the average value and therefore the cost of homes is somewhat lower than in the rest of the city ($458,194 in 2008 versus $524,000). At the same time, residential property values in East Somerville increased the most between 2003 and 2008 compared with the city overall (86 percent versus 80 percent). These property values in East Somerville contrast with those in West Somerville, which has the highest property values in the city (Office of the Mayor 2008: 7, 41).

East Somerville is also the site of the largest redevelopment project in Somerville, and this area is on the brink of very major change. Redevelopment is focused here because of a 145-acre, flat, open area called Assembly Square that fronts directly on the Mystic River and is immediately contiguous to Boston (see Assembly Square marked on the maps in this chapter). Its excellent highway access will soon to be enhanced by the creation of two new subway stops. This redevelopment (and its accompanying gentrification) is a source of both excitement (over new jobs and an expanded commercial tax base) and worry (over the loss of affordable housing) by East Somerville residents. It is also, as discussed in Chapter 3, a source of substantial civic engagement.

Economic Profile

A working-class identity has defined Somerville for well over a century, beginning with the establishment of late-nineteenth-century brickyards, a bleachery, a pottery plant, a gristmill, and a distillery. In the early to mid-twentieth century, the city saw meat-packing factories, dairy processing facilities, ice and food distributors, railroad yards, and the huge Ford Motor Company assembly plant that was completed in 1928, was closed in 1958, and is now the site of the huge Assembly Square development project.

In some respects, Somerville is still a working-class city—or at least it was in the years of my research—even though just 10 percent of city residents are employed in typical blue-collar jobs, such as operators, fabricators, or laborers (OSPCD 2009a). Another one-fifth (22 percent) of Somerville residents are employed in service roles, such as household, protective, craft, and repair workers, and another one-third (35 percent) are employed in technical support, sales, administrative support, and clerical support positions. Because workers in these jobs lack authority over others and have very little control over their own working conditions, sociologists often classify these jobs as working class (Hurst 2009: 16).

Using these categories, fully two-thirds of Somerville residents today are working class. As interviewee Sam Martin said, "There are no industrial jobs left, basically, so it's low-end service jobs . . . [and] I guess those are working-class jobs." As an economist who studied Somerville during its period of industrial decline argued, a "new working class [formed] composed of both blue collar and white collar workers" (Levenstein 1976: 28). Most people I interviewed told me that they see Somerville as still primarily a working-class city, although, as I discuss in later chapters, this claim may serve a political function.

Somerville today is also working class in the kind of employment available in the city. Most are lower-level service jobs. Top industries offer few professional or executive opportunities. Health and social services consist of ambulatory services, social assistance, nursing, and care facilities. Retail consists of small local stores, except for a Target, a Market Basket, and a Home Depot. Administrative and waste services and hotel and food services are also, for the most part, small and local. While small local establishments, especially stores and restaurants, are among Somerville's attractions and charms, they do not offer substantial numbers of high-paying jobs for local residents.

Housing patterns, income levels, and modes of transportation are also consistent with a working-class city. Somerville is a city of renters, with two-

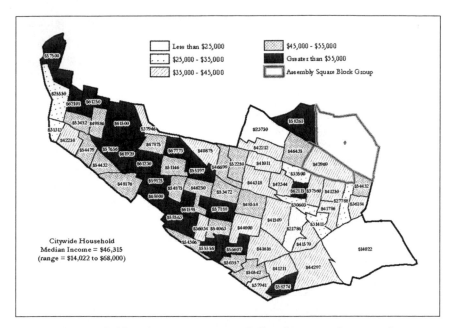

. **Figure 2.5.** Household Median Income, 2000. *(Office of Strategic Planning and Community Development [OSPCD],* Trends in Somerville: Population Technical Report *[Somerville, MA: City of Somerville, 2009], 66. Data from the U.S. Census.)*

thirds of residents renting instead of owning housing. The median household income among city residents in 2005 was $57,118, well below the median for the Greater Boston metropolitan area ($64,103) and somewhat lower than that for the state of Massachusetts in the same year ($59,059), but improved over that for 2000 ($46,315) (Figure 2.5). Reflective of an urban way of life, Somerville residents work close to home and rarely drive to work. The typical commute is under half an hour (24 minutes), and most commuters (51 percent) use public transportation (27 percent), walk to work or work at home (13 percent), or carpool (11 percent). One in four residents have no access to a car, truck, or van (data from the U.S. Census Bureau 2005).

When people in Somerville say that the city is becoming middle class, they mostly are referring to the rising cost of housing and to people who have moved out of the city because they can no longer afford to live there. Bruce Riley, who has lived all of his fifty years in Somerville and has risen to elected office, told me, "I think now Somerville is a middle-class city. . . . My daughter is currently looking for a house and she's not looking in Somerville because she can't afford it." In fact, the median value of owner-occupied housing units in Somerville doubled during just five short years between

2000 and 2005 from $214,100 to $435,200. Given that figure, it is not surprising that by 2005 one-half of owners with mortgages and nearly one-half of renters (44 percent) paid more than the recommended 30 percent of their income for housing.

By 2008, as in many cities, the average value of homes in Somerville had declined, even as city taxes on residential property increased (Hassett 2008d). Still, in 2008, the average home in the most affluent area of West Somerville was valued at $616,988. Here is where the rapid rise in housing costs has been most evident. This area includes Somerville's hip and lively Davis Square, which is connected by subway directly to Cambridge and then Boston. Less than a mile from Tufts University, Davis Square contains numerous popular restaurants, cafés, and arts-related small local businesses. This relatively affluent neighborhood is also the least racially diverse in the city, with the highest portion of the population identifying as white in 2000 (86 percent) compared with the city overall (77 percent) (Office of the Mayor 2008: 42). As former city appointee Richard Strickland, who lives in Davis Square, told me, "For those of us who moved in early, thirty years ago, we felt we were moving into a lower-middle-class community, and now, of course, we live in this much more grand kind of neighborhood, where there is a fair amount of money."

One-third (30 percent) of Somerville's residents are clearly middle- and upper-middle-class—that is, employed as executives, administrators and managers, or professional specialists. There has been, in recent years, a "constant influx of students and young professionals" reflected in the median age of thirty-one years recorded in the 2000 U.S. Census (OSPCD 2009b: 7). These young professionals who are choosing to make their home in Somerville reflect what urban sociologists call a new urban renaissance. This is marked by a rejection of suburban homogeneity, which is replaced with a cultural taste for urban diversity as a sign of cosmopolitan sophistication (Hannigan 1995; Lees 2008). When asked what kind of a place Somerville is, ten-year resident and Arts Council member Mark Lewis said:

> It's urban, close to Boston and Cambridge, but [it's] not like living *in* Boston. There are cafés and a lot of different kinds of restaurants. We also enjoy the mix of arts and the sort of working-class feel and the diversity. We could probably save $75,000 [buying a house in another town] just a mile away, but that's more suburban, less cultural.

Mark's description is echoed by the Boston metropolitan area newspaper's recent designation of Somerville as a Top Place to Live, emphasizing the arts community and its "loads of restaurants and bars, venues for indie music acts and film festivals" (Gehrman 2009: 15). I consider the gentrification of Somerville in Chapter 6.

City Government, History of Reform, and Local Civics and Politics Today

Throughout the mid-twentieth century, Somerville city government was characterized by political patronage, "insider politics" (Crowley 2009), corruption, and poor management. This began to improve in 1965 as "civic groups dissatisfied with their municipal government" organized, resulting in the election of a new mayor and the replacement of nine of the city's eleven aldermen (Fairclough 2009). In 1972, as a direct result of this organizing and the improvements it brought about, Somerville received its first All-America City award from the National Civic League (Crowley 2009), given for "efforts of citizens to install a reform government that exposed mismanagement of tax dollars, citing [the new mayor's] efforts to lead the government to be more responsive to community input" (Crowley 2009).

A recent grassroots history of this reform period, from 1966 to 1972, describes how "Housewives, school teachers, truck drivers, laborers, secretaries, senior citizens and some clergy just decided that they could change Somerville from what it had become into what they wanted it to be!" (Johnston 2009). Involved residents started new civic groups to gain influence in public affairs and initiated new city programs where none had existed before (preschools, teen centers, school lunch programs, elderly services, neighborhood health clinics). Perhaps the greatest effect of these reform groups came from residents' research into questionable spending of local tax revenues. It prompted the *Boston Globe* to conduct a Pulitzer Prize–winning investigation of graft by Somerville politicians.

The reformers of this period failed, however, in reaching one of their major goals: to block the construction of a major state-funded eight-lane highway that still cuts off east-side neighborhoods from the rest of Somerville and contributes to air and noise pollution. The reduced quality of life in this neighborhood because of this highway continues to be an occasion for civic action, just as it was over three decades ago.

While it is difficult to establish a direct causal relationship between the reform movement of the mid-1960s and early 1970s and the level of civic and political engagement by Somerville's residents today, some connections seem evident. Several of the civic groups mentioned in newspaper reports of that period have names very similar to those of groups that are important players in the city today. These include the earlier East Somerville Citizens for Action compared with today's East Somerville Neighbors for Change. The earlier Somerville Citizens for Adequate Transportation (SCAT), which unsuccessfully sued federal transportation authorities in 1966 to stop the eight-lane interstate highway, resembles today's Somerville Transportation Equity Partnership (STEP). The Somerville Corporation, established in 1969 "to create a community development corporation outside government," was apparently the precursor to today's Somerville Community Corps.

The city of Somerville is governed by a mayor who is elected to two-year terms and by an eleven-member Board of Aldermen. The mayor is the chief executive officer of the city and serves on the School Committee. The Board of Aldermen is the city's legislative branch. Members are elected every two years. Four members serve at large, and seven represent individual wards. The School Committee oversees the city's school system. It is composed of seven members elected by ward every two years. The mayor and the president of the Board of Aldermen serve as ex-officio voting members.

People who have lived in Somerville for a long time readily acknowledge the political corruption and bad government that are part of the city's legacy and challenge. Longtime resident Sean Russo, who is of Irish and Italian heritage, holds an elected office, and is considered a somewhat progressive member of the "old guard," told me:

> When I got out of the [military] service in 1974, Somerville had elected what some saw as a reform mayor. He was not of the old boy network. He openly took on the political corruption and the old boy network, and eventually he was driven out of office and one of the old boys was elected again. A reform mayor came in after that, and things have improved markedly since 1980.

Angela DeLuca's grandparents immigrated to Somerville from Italy. She has lived in the city her whole life and is now a leader in the business community. She said: "It was a challenge getting Somerville [businesses] more well known because there was a lot of bad connotation that went with the word Somerville. You can go back to the Winter Hill Gang. You can go back to all the bad politicians that were in this city, so we've cleaned up our act dramatically."

While certainly there have been significant improvements in the quality (and ethics) of city government since the reform movement, people I talked with called attention to the ongoing patronage they believe still characterizes Somerville politics. As Ted Nolan, a relative newcomer who once ran for city alderman, explained: "Somerville is kind of edging toward a more professional form of government, but there is still an expectation [that] city government [will] be a place where people can get jobs because they know someone. . . . [G]aining power means gaining friends in government." A number of people I talked with thought that the city patronage system, while it still holds sway to some extent, was slowly changing and provides an example of urban reform. Prominent active resident Dave Strong put it this way:

> Somerville has a municipal government that's somewhat of a typ-
> ical municipal machine. Every mayor used the city apparatus for
> patronage, to give jobs to supporters. . . . I like the mayor, but there's
> still the patronage thing. People still get jobs because of who they
> know. . . . But [there are] also a lot of people [now] who seem to be
> really qualified and brought in from the outside, more than in the
> previous administration. . . . The mayor has brought [in] a lot of peo-
> ple from the outside, people who didn't grow up here.

One public example of this movement away from local patronage was the mayor's decision in the summer of 2007 to hire a new chief of police, an African American from Florida. The chief, whom everyone I spoke with praised, won his new post over a longtime Somerville resident who had competed for the position.[5]

While there are some indications of change in who runs this city and how, in 2008 and 2009, the elected officials—mayor, aldermen, and School Committee—included not a single Latino, Haitian, or Asian member. The Somerville Office of the Mayor, as I have said, has been occupied for over eighty years by men (and one woman) of Irish and/or Italian heritage. Only one person of another ethnic group (a man of Portuguese descent) is remembered as having run for mayor during all that time. One woman of Portuguese heritage has served on the School Committee for a number of years. Everyone I talked to gave me virtually the same answer when I asked who runs the city now. Kevin Brennan, a youth leader of third-generation Irish background who was born and raised in the city, told me: "For the most part, the politicians in office right now are still from the old generation . . . still working class. . . . Most of the people in office have Irish or Italian heritage." Peter Evans, an active middle-aged progressive who has lived in the city for over two decades, concurred: "The power structure here is pretty much looking back a few generations to the people who were here in the forties and fifties. . . . I can only think of one alderman who isn't part of that." Vertus Bernique, a leader in the immigrant community who been a resident since the late 1980s, added race as a key factor in those who are elected to run the city: "The people are white, the white Somervillians who were born here, and even though their parents may be from another country, they feel they have ownership of the city. Those are the people who are the decision makers, the people who run the city." When asked about what kinds of power these political figures exercised, Kevin Brennan said: "[They] have the power to determine what gets built where . . . to determine contracts . . . to decide what parks get revitalized, what programs are going to be paid for, jobs in the recreation department and for youth, all these different things."

A commonly cited explanation for how the position of the "old guard" Democrats, with roots in the city's old, white, ethnic working class, has been perpetuated was expressed by Dave Strong:

> [According to] the city charter, the [city] elections are on the off years, so that only people who are really motivated, who work for the city or [have a] husband or friend [who] works for the city, people whose [city] jobs depend on it, those are the only people who come out and vote in any numbers. So that tends to lead to people electing the same sorts of people year after year. . . . The elections when lots of people come out, when there are state and national elections, are on the other years.

As a consequence of this system, I was told, Somerville-elected officials to the state legislature, in contrast to city officials, are from the more progressive, middle-class-identified wing of the Democratic party, while city officials tend to be more traditional blue-collar-identified "lunch bucket" Democrats.

Residents I talked with all told me that the city's power structure is homogeneous and that patronage, although waning, is still a driving factor in local politics. They defined their city as composed of diverse communities, and residents and city officials alike spoke to me about "the three Somervilles": (1) formerly working-class, lifelong, racially white Irish and Italian residents, sometimes called by themselves and others as "old school" or "old guard," now ironically themselves a kind of urban governing elite; (2) middle- and upper-middle-class, usually racially white young (and middle-aged) urban professionals, or "yuppies" to the lifelong residents, who—while they have many of the skills and attributes associated with civic and political engagement—are sometimes less committed to staying in the city once they have school-age children and are therefore perhaps less engaged; and (3) newer immigrants, often people of color, from Central and South America, the Caribbean, and Asia, frequently working class and low income, often non–English speakers, sometimes undocumented, who face the greatest difficulties in gaining a voice in public affairs. While these three groups are, of course, themselves internally diverse and the lines between them are not always sharp, they provide an overall snapshot of who lives in the city today.

Few individuals from the newer immigrant groups have stepped forward so far to run for political office, and those who have done so have fared badly. During the period of my research, a 2005 campaign by a young Latino man and a 2009 campaign by a well-respected local Latino businessman and local minister who had lived in the city for thirty years—both of whom ran for alderman—both ended in failure. The 2005 aldermen campaign turned ugly when hundreds of flyers were circulated the day before the election picturing a threatening-looking dark-skinned teenage male wearing a hooded sweatshirt and posed (in what was clearly a digitized image) alongside the Latino candidate. The flyer's text asked if voters wanted as alderman someone who associated with gangs in city hall. Flyers were dropped off at (among other locales) the city's elderly housing developments, playing directly into older (heavily voting) residents' fears about Latino gangs in the city. No investigation of who was responsible ever occurred, no one ever came forward, and when I spoke with the longtime incumbent who won the election, he expressed little interest in or concern about the event.

So today, eight decades after the election of John Murphy signaling the demise of the Yankee business elite and the rise of the white ethnic working class, those now middle-class descendants of that class have become an entrenched power. As I discuss further in Chapter 7, what I believe underlies much of the civic and political engagement in Somerville is the desire on the part of the two "newcomer" groups –non-immigrant middle-class professionals and the immigrant groups of the past twenty or so years— to change the face of elected leaders, to challenge what they see as the city's "old guard" of elected city officials, and to open up the process officials use to make decisions about the city's future. Major economic development projects and accompanying concerns about gentrification and displacement provide the arena for political struggle around this issue, and that is the topic of Chapter 3.

3

Major Redevelopment, Community Involvement, and Shared Governance

> In Somerville, people like to be involved. . . . In a lot of other places, you go to zoning hearings and nobody shows up. Here they're packed. . . . People live very close together in Somerville . . . [and] there's been this push for more transparency and more public hearings and more involvement. (Scott Mead, fifteen-year resident and local business leader)

Ted Nolan, who once ran for political office, spoke similarly: "There is a lot of activism [in the city] around public transportation, affordable housing, open space, building a stronger tax base. [And] there is increasing activism on the part of some of the [newer] ethnic communities about being more involved in the community."

This chapter explores how collective civic engagement most often takes place in Somerville through the vehicle of key voluntary associations. This engagement occurs within a larger framework of two kinds of struggles. One is about what I call social citizenship, that is, about which city residents are fully accepted into the public life of this urban community and which are not. The other is about the extent to which city officials and civic actors participate in the making of public decisions in terms of what I call shared governance. I explain both of these concepts in Chapter 1.

This chapter examines key arenas, sites, and issues around which active engagement was occurring during the period of my research. The voluntary associations[1] I discuss in this chapter are directly involved in the politics of power and conflict. Their actions relate to the debate I outlined at the beginning of this book about whether voluntary associations should become involved in the contentious realm of politics or focus instead on more consensus-oriented forms of engagement. The associations I dealt with in my research see influencing and interacting with local government as essential to improving the quality of life for residents. In the language of scholars who have developed typologies of ways that associations engage politically, these associations "create avenues for direct participation . . . in public governance or political resistance" (Fung 2003a: 516, 517). They interact with formal state structures as a way to constitute governance (Mark E. Warren 2001). This is in vivid contrast to a view of voluntary associations as largely apolitical social spaces that remain outside the rough-and-tumble environment of politics, separating themselves from conflict and the struggle for and exercise of power (Theiss-Morse and Hibbing 2005; Walker 2008).

Somerville's voluntary associations are especially active around perhaps the most important issue in urban politics: expanding the economic base of the city through urban development (Berry 2003: 115). As longtime active Somerville resident Dave Strong told me in a typical statement, "Almost all the big issues [in this city] are around development."

The term development in the context of U.S. urban settings refers mainly to the creation of housing, business and commercial property, and jobs for local residents (Frisch and Servon 2006; Markusen and Glasmeier 2008; Melendez and Servon 2007). The creation of affordable housing is often, as it is in Somerville, a main activity of community development organizations. These organizations may also mobilize local residents to become actively involved in development issues, thrusting them into the role of agents of civic participation (Silverman 2005).[2] One way Somerville's community development agency, the Somerville Community Corporation (SCC), does this is by sponsoring and providing staffing and other resources for two of the grassroots voluntary associations considered here: the Affordable Housing Organizing Committee (AHOC) and East Somerville Neighbors for Change (ESNC).

This chapter explains how key voluntary associations have been actively involved in public decisions around major redevelopment sites and projects in Somerville: the Mystic View Task Force (MVTF) and ESNC, focused on Assembly Square; the Somerville Transportation Equity Partnership (STEP), the AHOC, and Union Square Neighbors (USN), all focused on Union Square; and a coalition of four associations and organizations calling themselves the Community Corridor Planning (CCP) coalition, focused on the new subway Green Line.

My focus here is on collective action by voluntary associations. I aim to understand when they are able to influence city government and public decision making—sometimes becoming part of that decision making—and to what effect. My telling of how these voluntary associations became at times involved in actual public decision making shows that (1) civic actors can do more than influence government by also becoming part of actual shared governance and (2) civic actors can retain their independence from government by exercising their capacity to determine when to collaborate with government and when to act as separate agents or adversaries. This allows them to avoid being co-opted and losing autonomy by working too closely with government (Ostrander 2012).

As I note in Chapter 1, the absence of a strong urban regime in Somerville likely contributes to residents' efforts to create a public space for civic and political involvement through voluntary associations—although this space is more open to some residents than to others. Proponents of urban regime theory, a dominant theory of urban politics, have argued that power relations in cities play out largely between business and political elites (DeGaetano and Strom 2003; Mossberger and Stoker 2001; Stone 1993). The election in 1929 of the first Democratic mayor in Somerville marked the end of what, in 1870, a local newspaper had called the city's "ruling elite of Yankee businessmen" (Ueda 1987: 61). Since then, Somerville has lacked a strong, politically engaged business elite, and until recently, its city government has been weakened by a parochial and familial system of private patronage as well as being characterized by periods of corruption. Under the current mayor, the city administration is moving away from this private patronage to a "good government" approach that includes aggressively increasing commercial and real estate development in the city (Gottdiener and Hutchison 2006: 234).

City Hall in Somerville today is pushing for increased commercial and real estate development, largely because it will alleviate the city's heavy reliance on residential property taxes and (declining) monies from the state of Massachusetts. In the city's 2009 budget, three-quarters comes from residential property taxes, a high rate compared with surrounding cities and towns. As MVTF leader Ted Nolan said, "One of [our] biggest problems is the tax base. Somerville doesn't have the resources it needs to address the needs of residents." Sheila Gayner agreed: "Our tax base is really a disaster. We don't have enough commercial development here to support the services the city needs, and so we end up getting a lot of money from state aid. . . . We have to improve that. I really think it holds the city back."

In addition to the ongoing problem of the tax base, in 2009 alone, Somerville suffered a loss of just over one-fourth (27 percent) of its state-level funding (Abel 2009). This, of course, makes creating new Somerville-based commercial revenue all the more important.

City Hall's push for more commercial development also offers an important occasion in Somerville, as it does in other urban contexts, for civic and political engagement. While Somerville residents welcome the potential for increased commercial tax revenues and the relief this would provide for their property taxes, at the same time, many also resist growth strategies that threaten both their own ability to continue to live in the city and city's class and ethnic diversity. As engaged residents support economic development, they also want to ensure that city officials protect low-income and working-class residents and preserve the city's heritage of welcoming new immigrants and valuing the working class. The *Somerville News* described this attitude of local residents, as displayed at a community meeting held in July 2008, as "tensely ambivalent . . . expressing both their optimism . . . and their fears," especially of resident displacement (Federico 2009a).

My interviews provide evidence of substantial levels of civic engagement around redevelopment projects that are changing the city enormously. Peter Evans, a leader in several organizations, said, "It is a city where there is a lot of ability to participate and influence and change things." Sheila Gayner agreed: "It's small enough that you feel you can make a difference." Suggesting that both the city's relatively small geographic area (four square miles) and its high density are reasons for resident engagement, business leader Scott Mead stated, "People [here] care more. People live in very close quarters. You're rubbing up against your neighbors a lot." Dave Strong, who, after years of civic activism, now occupies an elected post, told me, "The reason I love it here is that people are really involved in the community. There are a lot of different kinds of community groups." Newer immigrant groups—as I discuss in Chapter 5—have had a more difficult time in entering this space, but even in the face of obstacles, they do participate in public life, although, as immigrant advocate Steve Smith described to me, "more [as] a client group than [as] power." This is a very important example of how newer immigrants in the city are excluded from what I call here social citizenship and therefore also from shared governance.

Somerville civic actors told me that most of the current involvement of residents during the years of this study was taking place specifically around two main development sites in the city. Assembly Square is a 145-acre flat, open site on the Mystic River and the Boston city line, and Union Square is a busy, highly trafficked potential arts and ethnic cultural center with historical roots in sites from Revolutionary War times. In addition to these two sites, the coming of the new subway Green Line is a catalyst for a great deal of talk and action both by civic actors and by city government. I devote a section of this chapter to each of these three major issues and sites of engagement.

These two main development sites are critically important to the future of the city. Assembly Square is the former site of an enormous Ford Motor assembly plant that closed in 1958 and since the 1970s has been occupied by a deteriorating shopping mall. Plans for this huge, flat, virtually unoccupied area along the Mystic River, closest to the Boston city border, include a large IKEA store and a new subway station that will enhance an existing subway line (the Orange Line), bringing people more easily to and from Boston and across Somerville. Union Square is a multi-ethnic, mixed working- and middle-class proposed new city center. Union Square will profoundly change in the next decade, with the arrival of a subway line planned to begin construction in 2012 and open in 2014 (Guha 2009c). This project was recently delayed until 2018 (Byrne 2011). Now that the 2008 major street reconstruction to ease the square's longtime, locally famous traffic bottleneck is complete, local leaders hope that people from around the area who may previously have avoided the square will be attracted by a lively scene of ethnic restaurants and shops, an arts center, and the like.

Contested Site One—Assembly Square:
New Open Space, Enhanced Commercial Tax Base,
and New Jobs for Residents

In addition to the widely recognized need to expand the city's commercial tax base, another goal of the Assembly Square redevelopment is job creation, which many see as key to retaining the city's working-class population. As Nolan continued, "Somehow we have to find ways to both increase employment opportunities and also do a better job preparing folks for the kinds of employment that will enable them to afford to stay here."

The Somerville civic association that has had perhaps the greatest effect on how Assembly Square will be developed is the MVTF, named for the Mystic River, which borders this large tract of land. The MVTF convened in the summer of 1998, with the specific aim of establishing a public process for future development of the Assembly Square area (Mystic View Task Force n.d.). At that time, in the view of people I spoke with, city officials were taking very little account of resident's concerns.

During the 1990s, the Assembly Square Mall, which had replaced the closed Ford factory, was failing. Neighboring industrial sites were vacant, and a series of development proposals had come to nothing. People who attended task force meetings were interested in Assembly Square's redevelopment as a way to improve Somerville's economy and tax base. Some also focused on creating recreational opportunities along the Mystic River. Most sought a mixed-use development to replace the current big box stores and parking lots.

Members of the MVTF (residents, businesspeople, and a handful of local politicians) met regularly during 1998 and 1999. On May 22, 1999, they organized a community forum called Somerville's Last Frontier. Over 150 people attended, including the city's then-mayor. The forum resulted in a vision of a pedestrian-oriented, mixed-use development that could potentially provide acres of usable open space; diverse, high-quality jobs; and over $30 million in new net tax revenue (MVTF n.d.).

When it failed to get the city administration to listen and respond to that vision, the MVTF joined with the Conservation Law Foundation to bring a legal suit against the city of Somerville. The suit contended that the Somerville Planning Board had failed to call for public hearings and traffic studies when they issued permits in 2000 for a huge Home Depot store (Chabot 2002a, 2002b). When a local court ruled in favor of the task force in September 2002, the MVTF became a key player to whom city officials and developers now had to listen. In April 2003, the battle continued, with the city arguing, contrary to the community vision created earlier, that Assembly Square was large enough to accommodate both Home Depot and the planned IKEA store. The MVTF then sued again to prevent the building of two big box stores that they argued would generate high levels of traffic and pollution and insufficient jobs for residents (Mystic View Task Force n.d.).

In January 2004, the newly elected mayor announced that Assembly Square was his number one priority. His actions over the next few months and into the next year indicated a change in posture toward community input into the planning. As the stalemate over the 2003 lawsuit continued, the mayor called a press conference in May 2004 to say that he had obtained funding from the U.S. Department of Housing and Urban Development (HUD) to revitalize Assembly Square. A few months later, in September 2004, the city issued building permits for the construction. On October 31, 2005, during a ribbon-cutting ceremony for a new Christmas Tree Shop in the Square, the mayor announced that he had "broken the logjam" by making a deal with developers to incorporate community concerns about affordable housing, open space, and better pedestrian access.

The desire by the new mayor to claim credit for negotiating a deal with developers that took account of residents' wishes signaled a shift in the city's willingness to establish what the MVTF had originally set out to create: a more open public process around the development of Assembly Square.

In April 2006, further negotiations with IKEA led to an agreement to move its planned store away from the Mystic River, freeing up sixteen acres for a new riverfront park. Worn down by the task force's success with legal appeals and seeking a more collaborative and less oppositional relationship with the MVTF, key developer Federal Realty Investment Trust (FRIT) and IKEA entered into direct negotiations with the MVTF in June 2006.

In August 2006, the state of Massachusetts law appeals division sided with Somerville residents who had argued three years earlier that the Massachusetts Department of Environmental Protection should not have issued a license to IKEA to build on the river in the first place (Reidy 2006). On October 17, 2006, the MVTF, FRIT, and the mayor announced that all three parties had reached a settlement of their long-standing disputes. The agreement, signed in December 2006, stated that FRIT would take steps to guarantee long-term development that would provide more jobs and tax revenue to the city than their initial retail and residential projects had entailed. The developers also agreed to specific steps to mitigate the environmental effects of increased traffic and to improve public open space along the Mystic River and throughout the site. In return, the task force agreed to drop its pending lawsuits and not to bring future ones.

Most importantly for my argument that the MVTF had achieved a level of civic participation that constituted actual shared governance, the legal agreement explicitly stated that, "A body consisting of appointees from the neighborhoods, the City of Somerville, and Mystic View will supervise development of the short and long term plans" (Mystic View Task Force 2006).

The new mayor, at the same time as he announced the three-way agreement, also announced that U.S. Congressman Mike Capuano (a former Somerville mayor) had obtained $25 million for a new Assembly Square subway station. In January 2007, all parties, now collaborating, signed a final document to limit the negative environmental consequences of proposed development and to ensure that initial retail development makes way for more valuable mixed-use development in the future. Three months later, in April 2007, all parties agreed to a new off-river IKEA site, with IKEA putting in a $15 million supplement to federal money for the new subway station.

Ted Nolan, MVTF leader, described past activities and accomplishments this way:

> I think that the community felt that city government was acceding to the interests of developers who would have been content to

develop Assembly Square as a big box [store] center. We felt that was squandering one of the most important potential sources of tax revenues and jobs and open space for the city. What was really frustrating was that the city appeared to be having open meetings, but when the plans were made, they seemed to basically reflect what the developers wanted. . . . The Mystic View Task Force . . . felt like its only resort was to sue to stop it . . . and that's what we did. There were two efforts to mediate the dispute, and those failed because I think the developers didn't go to the table in good faith because they felt like they were promised by the city that they would get what they wanted and they didn't really have to accede to the demands of the community. The last time mediation was proposed, it was a much more serious effort. A high-profile mediator . . . who had been an environmental activist as well as a state government leader, played the role of mediator. A new group of developers took it more seriously. I think the community also realized this was a real opportunity to negotiate a meaningful solution . . . and we were able to reach an agreement.

While the MVTF's actions were controversial at the time, once agreement had been reached, even leaders of Somerville's business community acknowledged that the plans for Assembly Square had turned out well. When asked to name groups in the city that could make things happen, lifelong Somerville resident and prominent business leader Angela DeLuca said:

Well, there was this incredible group down in Assembly Square. They stopped the development. Mystic View [Task Force], they stopped it dead in the water. . . . It is absolutely for the better. . . . We didn't end up with a lot of big boxes. We are ending up with some very nice retail. We are ending up, hopefully, if the [real estate] climate ever changes, with some very nice residential property down there. The tax base is going to increase.

In March 2009, U.S. Senator John Kerry from Massachusetts assured local leaders that federal money for development of the area was still forthcoming, even in light of the by-then national financial crisis. While the eventual completion of current plans for Assembly Square and East Somerville's redevelopment is years off,[3] what is certain is that a key grassroots voluntary association, the MVTF, became a central political player with whom city officials and developers found they needed to be in regular active negotiation.

In November 2009, the MVTF also joined with the city's Comprehensive Plan Steering Committee (SomerVision), working to prepare for the subway Green Line extension and its effect on development and other issues around the city. This was a continuation of its move from an oppositional to a collaborative relationship with city government, with the potential for actively governing instead of a role limited to influencing city officials.

A second civic association that played a role in the development of Assembly Square is ESNC. While the MVTF focused on land use, recreational space, and transportation issues, ESNC is most concerned that the new Assembly Square will mean jobs for city residents. ESNC formed in the spring of 2003 under the auspices of the SCC, the city's community development agency. In October 2007, after a grassroots community visioning process that attracted over 350 residents, the group voted to support an East Somerville Action Plan (Hassett 2007a) that gave the highest ranking to "community benefits campaigns for jobs at Assembly Square" (Somerville Community Corporation n.d.).

By January 2008, prompted by ESNC and SCC staff, the city and IKEA had signed a formal agreement stating that IKEA would contribute $100,000 for an employment training program for Somerville residents so they could compete for jobs at the new IKEA, would give the city six computers to make IKEA's online application process accessible to Somerville residents, would place ads in the two Somerville newspapers for four weeks to recruit new workers, and would give those in East Somerville first opportunity to apply during a specified two-week period, with multi-lingual flyers announcing this opportunity to be distributed by the city to homes in this area. At successive SCC and ESNC meetings I attended in the summer and fall of 2008, a main topic among members was their continued discussions with the mayor about implementing this agreement to ensure that East Somerville residents actually were hired when the new IKEA opened. Both SCC and the mayor lay claim to making the agreement with IKEA to help Somerville residents apply for new jobs.[4]

Contested Site Two—Union Square:
A New Subway Line, Affordable Housing,
and a Commercial and Cultural Center

Union Square is the city's oldest and largest commercial area, zoned as a central business district and known in the metropolitan Boston area for its diverse, affordable, and ethnically varied restaurants and markets (Office of Housing and Community Development 2002: 8). Other Union Square destinations include the post office, the public safety building, a popular flower market, charter and elementary schools, and banks. Changes in Union Square have produced a community of new immigrant families, long-term residents, students, authors, artists, and young professionals. The area is also a historic Revolutionary War site, and the First Grand Union Flag was raised atop Union Square's Prospect Hill on January 1776. Paul Revere passed through this area on his historic ride, alerting colonists to the Redcoats' arrival in Boston in April 1775.

Everyone interviewed recognized that, as young, third-generation Somerville native Kevin Brennan told me, "Union Square is going to be a whole different place in ten or fifteen years."[5] Most people said that Union Square's development should balance the city's multiple needs for commercial tax revenues, affordable housing, and a new vibrant cultural center. Peter Evans, active MVTF member, told me, "I would like to see Union Square be a place that is not just a thriving commercial center but also a community center."

The major issues in the redevelopment of Union Square are horrendous traffic congestion, a long-promised new subway line stop, affordable housing, and the height of new commercial buildings intended to enhance the area as a new city center. The city's arts community has designated Union Square as a place to live and work, supported by the city administration's understanding that artists can be important for urban development (Zukin 2009). Civic associations that have entered into the debates around these various issues are the Somerville Transportation Equity Partnership (STEP), formed in June 2003; the Affordable Housing Organizing Committee (AHOC), founded in June 2001; and the small but vocal Union Square Neighbors (USN), formed in 2006.

In contrast to how city administrations in the 1990s had shut out city residents from the initial planning for Assembly Square—influencing the MVTF's decision to sue the city to get the attention of officials and to be taken seriously by them—the planning for Union Square was, from the outset, a more open process. During 2001 and 2002, for example, Somerville's Office of Housing and Community Development held public meetings that culminated, only after considerable resident input, in an area Master Plan adopted by the city's Board of Aldermen. As Ted Nolan said, "The process of debating Union Square development and zoning . . . is as open and inclusive . . . as I can imagine. The process has been much more inclusive than previous planning efforts. . . . In Assembly Square . . . the developers who had purchased the property had disproportionate influence." As Deb Morris, five-year resident newcomer and leader in Somerville's progressive political organization, put it, "[With] Union Square zoning . . . [the city] is doing a really good job listening to people's concerns. The Assembly Square zoning was a complete mess, and they didn't listen."

A key voluntary association shaping the new Union Square is the STEP, a (501)(c)(4) advocacy organization. While Union Square is not the only focus of STEP's work, this organization has devoted substantial effort to the extension of the regional subway Green Line into Union Square. This aspect of Union Square's development will create the greatest change, not only in Union Square but also throughout Somerville. I tell more of the Green Line story in the next section of this chapter.

Located at the intersection of several major arterials that provide a cross-town and regional highway system, Union Square's streets are typically grid-locked during the morning and afternoon rush hours with the cars and buses that make it a mass transit hub (Office of Housing and Community Development 2002: 45). Sheila Gayner told me:

> When I moved to Somerville, I was shocked [by] how difficult it is to get across Somerville. Having lived in [other local towns] where they have great transportation, it just offended me. I started to research and realized that [the state] promised to build the [new subway] Green Line in 1990 and it never happened, so I sought out some people and [we organized].

Strategies used by the STEP were able to be more collaborative compared with the more oppositional strategies that the MVTF found they had to use to get the city administration's attention. As Gayner explained:

> We made a very strong case for bringing the Green Line to Somerville through reaching out to the community and having people write letters to the Metropolitan Planning Committee and actually having them take us very seriously, then having the MBTA [Massachusetts Bay Transportation Authority] and the Executive Office of Transportation come to Somerville for a hearing. Then the community [and] the elected officials began to take us more seriously . . . and see us as helpful advocates.

According to my interviews with STEP leaders and my review of online minutes of regular monthly meetings of STEP from January 2005 to March 2009, strategies included constantly monitoring and reporting about policy decisions at state, regional, and federal levels that affect their areas of interest; attending public meetings and hearings at state and local levels and speaking out for STEP priorities; bringing relevant city department heads into their membership, with the aim of collaborating on shared goals; meeting with state and local officials; and working with like-minded groups in the contiguous towns of Cambridge and Medford. STEP members also used flyers and other forms of communication to get residents to attend public meetings, and they staffed booths at community events (such as Somerville's annual Art Beat summer street festival and farmer's markets around the city) to educate local residents about transportation issues and STEP's aims and activities. STEP also reaches out to non-member residents to solicit views of the larger community. They partner with other Somerville organizations and conduct periodic resident surveys in multiple languages to use in their advocacy.

A second Somerville association engaged in shaping the new Union Square is the AHOC, founded in 2001 and staffed and organized by the SCC. Described by a national group of urban thinkers and leaders in 2004 as a "motley crew of neighborhood activists" (Agarwal 2004), the AHOC describes itself as a group of Somerville tenants, homeowners, and local agency representatives devoted to preserving and increasing housing opportunities in Somerville. While it took the AHOC several years to get organized, by 2004, it was ready for its first campaign: to increase the amount of money, called linkage fees, developers had to pay to the city's affordable housing trust fund in exchange for building permits and zoning ordinances. The AHOC uses classic grassroots organizing methods, going door-to-door for "one-on-one" conversations with city residents to mobilize support. Next, the AHOC collaborated with a progressive member of the Board of Aldermen, who agreed to introduce the AHOC's proposal, once convinced that this group had broad support. In November 2004, the AHOC scored an attention-getting victory when the Board of Aldermen adopted its hard-fought proposal to increase the linkage fees.

Like the STEP, the AHOC's activities are not limited to Union Square, but that area has been a major focus of its work. While the AHOC supports the redevelopment of Union Square and its establishment as a city arts destination, this group has been concerned that the city's plan leaves behind low- and middle-income families. When city officials unveiled a plan in November 2006 to rezone Union Square to provide incentives to developers to build housing and work spaces for artists, the AHOC promptly held a press conference calling for more affordable housing units. A short while later, the AHOC brought a proposal to the Board of Aldermen asking that 15 percent of new housing be designated as affordable instead of the required 12.5 percent (Green 2006).

A third voluntary association, USN, formed in 2006 in response to the city plan being considered at that time to raise the height of buildings in Union Square to what USN considered unacceptable levels. Their concern was that increased building height would alter the scale and neighborhood feel of Union Square and block sunlight. They asked, "Would shopping at the Union Square Farmer's Market be the same in the shadow of twelve-story buildings?"

About fifteen residents made up the core of USN in 2006, and this group included among its members professional city planners (although not ones employed by the city of Somerville). The group attracted at least one member through their reputed "expertise and their ability to approach stakeholders in a spirit of collaboration" (Green 2007b). A USN posting in December 2008 on a community blog called Somerville Voices stated the group's position as follows:

> Our priority is to get the right balance between a vital, livable [Union] Square and creating new business and housing. We want to manage growth so it doesn't overwhelm the people and the businesses that are there now. . . . We know Somerville needs more tax revenue, but the city's plan seems to say Union Square is now going to be the epicenter of development for the whole city. We feel it can be part of the picture but not the only tax generator. We want to preserve the neighborhood and historic qualities of Union Square and build on those rather than throw them all to the side. (Somerville Voices n.d.)

In addition, USN noted the following points of contention with what the city and developers proposed: "On affordable housing, we would support more than the city's proposed 121/2 percent minimum but not as an excuse to build ever more height and density" (Somerville Voices n.d.)

As an indication that city officials were taking seriously resident input about Union Square, the Board of Aldermen chose not to act on the city administration's 2006 and 2007 proposals for Union Square to allow time for revisions incorporating resident concerns. At a June 2008 meeting, aldermen presented their proposed plan for Union Square and members of the AHOC and USN were vocal participants, as they were at a subsequent meeting later in 2008 (Hassett 2008c). A lifelong resident who was a youth activist expressed the view of residents who were both excited about new transportation and fearful of increases in the cost of housing when he said, "I can't wait to jump on the [new subway] Green Line. Then I say, 'Where am I gonna live?'" (Dreilinger 2008c).

In a substantial victory for the AHOC and other civic actors, on April 23, 2009, Somerville's Board of Aldermen finally approved a plan for Union Square that increased the required 12.5 percent of affordable housing to between 15 percent and 17 percent, depending on the area (Nash 2009b).[6] I see this process and its outcome as an important example of how public decisions can emerge as socially produced outcomes actively negotiated between governmental and non-governmental actors. This contrasts with a view of public decisions as acts solely by city government.

The next section of this chapter explores how a coalition of Somerville civic associations and organizations negotiated with local government in a different way. At first, they chose to act separately from the city and later moved toward greater collaboration. I discuss this briefly in Chapter 1 as a way for associations to retain their ability to work closely with government at times and to work independently at other times. This allows them to participate in what I call shared governance and still avoid the dangers of losing their autonomy in relation to government.

Subway Green Line Extension and a 2009 Comprehensive Community Visioning Process: Local Associations Collaborating (and Not) with City Government

The community voluntary associations discussed so far in this chapter use a variety of strategies to accomplish their goals. Whether their strategies are more oppositional or collaborative is shaped by a shifting political context in which city officials seem more or less open to association involvement, offering greater or fewer opportunities for engagement. When the city's process seems to offer genuine chances for civic input, associations are willing to collaborate. When civic actors see the local government's decision-making process as less than open, then these actors opt for more oppositional approaches.

Early oppositional strategies by the MVTF led to victory through legal suits. The MVTF's legal successes seemed to persuade city government to create a more negotiated decision-making process around Assembly Square, consistent with shared governance. When it came time later for the city to propose plans for redeveloping Union Square, the process the city chose was more open from the outset, and consequently, the strategies used by community associations could be less oppositional and more collaborative.

A key example of the city providing more opportunity for residents to be involved after the Assembly Square debacle was a community-wide visioning process that took place in Somerville throughout the spring, summer, and fall of 2009. A main focus of that visioning was to plan for the expected effect of the new subway Green Line. As the director of a key Somerville community organization put it, "The coming of the Green Line is going to dominate our lives for the next twenty years. We got it. Now we all need to work on how we want it to impact our community." Dick O'Neil, longtime elected city official, spoke also about how important the Green Line project is: "The whole reshaping of the city's image, the Green Line coming to Somerville is probably the biggest issue we're all focused on now."

When the city administration invited a coalition of local associations and nonprofit organizations to co-sponsor the city administration's visioning process, the community coalition declined. Instead, the coalition chose to pursue a parallel process of its own. I put this forward here as an example of civic actors making a strategic choice about when to collaborate with government and when to act separately and retain their autonomy and independence. The following description of these two parallel processes also provides a rich comparison of how an official government body operates compared with a grassroots community-based coalition when both engage in a similar project of developing a vision for their community's future.

The history of the commitment by the state of Massachusetts to extend the region's subway Green Line into Somerville, especially into Union Square, has been long and contested. It goes back to the 1920s, when the state's Metropolitan Planning Commission considered extending area trains into Somerville (Guha 2009a). While a complete telling of the Somerville Green Line saga over the past ninety years is not possible here, some background to the events of 2009 is useful. The importance of the Green Line to the city's redevelopment is often compared with the transformation of the city's Davis Square, where Somerville's only currently existing subway station opened in 1984. Once a declining area with boarded up stores, Davis Square today is a lively and attractive area of the city, and as described in Chapter 2, it is the most costly place in the city to live.

In 1990, the state of Massachusetts finally agreed to make good on its legal obligation to fund and build an extension of the Boston-area subway's Green Line into Somerville as payback for the pollution increase caused by Boston's notorious Big Dig highway project (Kaiser 2004). The state's agreement came only after the city successfully won the first of several lawsuits aimed at holding the state to this obligation. Ten years later, in 2000, no progress had been made, despite the state's legal commitment. This prompted the city of Somerville and the Conservation Law Foundation to file another lawsuit. In 2006, this litigation, with the help of community support and advocacy groups, such as the STEP and the Union Square Task

Force, finally brought about a multi-million-dollar state investment in the Green Line extension.

During 2004 and 2005, hundreds of Somerville residents attended public hearings to convince state officials of the merits of the Green Line extension. The mayor kept pressing the point that "the state has made a legal commitment to this project and it must follow through" (City of Somerville 2005a). Advocates emphasized the finding by the state's own transportation agency that the new subway line would cut automobile traffic by 64,000 vehicles a day and the Somerville Chamber of Commerce claim that it would bring three billion dollars in economic activity to the city (City of Somerville 2005b).

By August 2008, the local newspaper reported, "The Green Line is coming to Somerville; that is definite. However where it will stop is not" (Nicas 2008b). Negotiations between the city and the state transportation authorities continued about exactly where the Green Line stops would be built. The Union Square stop was especially contested because it would require a spur off the main line.

The mayor reported, "The state remains strongly committed to completing the project by 2014," but a potential roadblock was where to place a large maintenance facility that the state agency was threatening to locate in an empty plot of land near Assembly Square called the Inner Belt. The city wanted to preserve this area for future development (Curtatone 2008). The mayor appealed, as he often did, to the city's need to "expand our commercial tax base and reduce burden on our hard-pressed residential taxpayers" (Curtatone 2008). The state eventually backed off its threat and agreed to build the maintenance facility elsewhere.[7]

Shortly thereafter, the city and the earlier mentioned coalition of community organizations both announced their parallel "community visioning" processes, both of which would begin in the spring of 2009 and continue throughout the end of the year. The city's process was named SomerVision. While the Green Line was not the only focus, it was a main one. SomerVision kicked off on Saturday, April 25, 2009, with an afternoon open house held at a public school cafeteria. People mingled, looking at maps and plans displayed for Assembly Square; Union Square; East Somerville's main thoroughfare, Broadway; and the proposed route for the Green Line. All materials came from city offices, with the exception of one booth that was staffed and developed by STEP.

During the couple of hours I spent at the open house, perhaps twenty people other than those staffing the city displays walked around, looking at booths with the displays. With few exceptions, the crowd was white and apparently Anglo. A short film depicting the history of bringing the Green Line to Somerville was shown. The mayor arrived to applause and mounted the stage for a short speech, saying in part, "We're trying to build up the neighborhoods . . . to bring back the neighborhoods . . . to make Somerville a place to bring families who will want to stay . . . to reclaim areas and bring new neighborhoods there."

At around this same time in the spring of 2009, the Office of the Mayor announced a series of ten public "information sessions on key trends occurring within Somerville" (text of flyer) intended to feed in to SomerVision. These sessions were held at various venues around the city between May and October 2009, and Somerville's Office of Strategic Planning and Community Development led them. People I interviewed offered praise for the openness and transparency of its relatively new director, who had come from Oakland, California, and Washington, D.C., and who was appointed by the mayor in 2007. Like the police chief from Florida, her appointment from outside the city was a departure from local custom.

One of the information sessions I attended in May 2009 focused on population trends. A young city staffer explained that the series would "provide a fact-based foundation for . . . projects to improve the City of Somerville" (van der Heiden 2009). About twenty people sat in chairs arranged in rows in another school cafeteria. The project manager showed a PowerPoint presentation with informative charts and graphs and invited questions and comments. There were a few: a suggestion to look at trends in surrounding areas to see their potential effect on Somerville, an expression of concern about an under-counting of newer immigrant groups, a question about the effect of the 1980 Red Line subway stop on Davis Square, and a question (unanswered) about how these data would be used by the city to make decisions.

On April 29, 2009, in the same school cafeteria where the city had held its SomerVision open house just four days earlier, the coalition of civic associations and organizations held their first community meeting on a Wednesday evening from 6:00 p.m. to 8:00 p.m. They called themselves the Community Corridor Planning coalition (CCP): "a grassroots non-profit coalition committed to resident participation in planning for a livable, equitable, Somerville" (text from flyer). The group included STEP, the city's community development agency the SCC, a small organization focused on environmental issues called Groundwork Somerville, and the city's health alliance. In an apparent nod toward shared governance, the city's SomerVision project manager and his co-leader also spoke at the coalition's evening event. They said, "We see ourselves as partners with you in the beginning stages of a city-wide plan."

About seventy people attended the CCP community meeting, which was described by the welcoming speaker as "the first of many." It appeared that about one-third of those present were Latino, Brazilian, or Haitian, in vivid contrast to the city's largely white Anglo attendees. The flyers publicizing the coalition event were in multiple languages, and interpreters (multi-lingual Somerville youth trained by the local immigrant advocacy organization called the Welcome Project) provided translation into Spanish, Portuguese, and Haitian Creole. The introductory speaker identified the goal of the meeting as to "ensure that the Green Line meets the needs of our diverse communities." She told those assembled that the evening's discussion would be compiled and used in the next stage of CCP's process, a series of small gatherings held in residents' homes over the summer. A culminating meeting would occur in October, where participants would develop principles to guide a community vision that would be conveyed to city decision makers.

Most of the April CCP meeting was spent in small group activities as people sat in groups of ten or so at tables labeled with the names of planned Green Line stops around the city. Led by volunteer facilitators, participants at each table (including me) named places they especially liked in the area of the stop and said what would make the area better, what their worries were about the changes the Green Line would bring, and what could be done to address these concerns.

At one of the summer small gatherings, someone asked why CCP had decided not to include city officials. A coalition leader responded that the community process was meant to run in parallel with the city's initiative and stated that CCP would share the proposals that emerged from their grassroots process once they adequately represented the concerns and wishes of the community (Maislin 2009).

The culminating October CCP meeting was again held on a Wednesday evening. A buffet meal was provided. I counted about a hundred people present, about half of whom appeared to be Latino, Brazilian, or Haitian. Translation was again provided by youth from the Welcome Project. The opening speaker from one of the CCP organizations talked about the city administration's ongoing separate comprehensive planning process, saying, "We can influence that plan. We can say to them what we want." The same two city staffers who had spoken at the April meeting were present, but did not speak this time.

The plan for the evening was to develop and then prioritize a set of principles to guide the city's vision, first at each table, and then as the whole group. Discussions started with a list of sixteen principles generated from the series of summer small gatherings. At the end of the evening, once all the groups at the tables had put forth their priorities and those priorities were voted on by the entire assembly, final core principles were as follows (not in any rank order). Shortly after the meeting, CCP issued a document (in English, Spanish, Portuguese, and Haitian Creole) aimed both at influencing the city's vision and framing the agenda for active civic engagement by city residents for the next few years.

> As part of the work of Community Corridor Planning, a grassroots initiative to engage Somerville residents in the land use planning of the Green Line Corridor, community members ratified a list of eleven core principles. The principles listed here were chosen from a larger list of principles generated by over 300 residents who participated at various community meetings held between April and October, 2009, which were then prioritized and ratified at a community meeting attended by 150 people on October 28, 2009. The community members engaged with CCP would like to see all decisions related to the planning of the Green Line and the land use in the half mile areas around the 7 proposed stations to reflect this list of Corridor Core Principles.

- *More Local Jobs:* We want a fixed percentage of respectable jobs of all types with good wages and benefits for Somerville residents, from construction to permanent.
- *Increase Commercial and Economic Development:* We want to see the creation of squares as destinations, with careful attention to mixed use of commercial/residential, reuse of buildings, and economic development to increase the tax base.
- *Keep and Add Local Businesses:* We want locally owned, culturally diverse, clean businesses in commercial areas with employees who live in Somerville.
- *Keep Somerville Affordable:* We want to make sure people of all economic means have the ability to afford housing and living costs, so that Somerville residents, such as child care workers, cab drivers, local business employees and others can stay here affordably.
- *Maintain Our Diversity:* Preserve and encourage economic and ethnic diversity of residents and businesses.
- *Improve the Green Environment:* We want a safe, environmentally friendly neighborhood with more green space, trees, and gardens; reduction of noise; avoidance of light pollution; and prevention of toxic chemicals in the air.

- *Encourage Walking and Biking:* We want to encourage walking and cycling, through safe, bike/pedestrian friendly design of streets and paths around and between stations.
- *Create Community Gathering Spaces:* We want both indoor and outdoor safe, public gathering spaces for community members.
- *Improve Access:* We want above standard, safe access to and between stations for people with disabilities, strollers, and pedestrians in general.
- *Community Involvement:* We want to make sure residents are included on an ongoing basis in the planning, design, and zoning changes to the stations and areas around them. Youth, artists, and others should help design stations, with attention to amenities. We need an easy and clear process for residents to address problems as they come up, with ways of immediately resolving unseen impacts.
- *Connecting Buses and Trains:* We want to ensure inter-modal access between neighborhoods and stations, for new train service to be adequate and speedy, and for existing bus lines to continue to serve areas not connected by train. (Community Corridor Planning 2009)

Meanwhile, in September 2009 the mayor appointed a sixty-member comprehensive plan steering committee that included several of the same individuals who led CCP. He charged the committee with reviewing resident input from the SomerVision meeting to begin drafting a city vision for the next two decades. After several city-sponsored smaller meetings in December 2009, SomerVision called a large public meeting attended by about one hundred people on January 5, 2010. This gathering was run according to a process developed by a national consulting group called the World Café (http://www.theworldcafe.com/). Urged by the immigrant advocacy organization the Welcome Project, this time the city also offered multiple simultaneous language translations. The program consisted of a series of structured "conversations" held at each of eighteen tables of six persons each. First, the participants told where in the city they lived and/or worked, for how long, what they liked most, and what made Somerville special for them. Then there was a change of tables. The next set of questions was about what the participants wanted Somerville to be twenty years in the future, what the city was "best at," and what concerns were commonly shared. A "report out" to the full assembly from each table gave one priority that the participants wanted to conserve for the future, one possibility, and one concern. Priorities that were identified included keeping the small town feel and keeping local businesses. For possibilities, the participants suggested making areas of the city free of automobiles. Concerns identified by the participants included how to turn the city's diversity into democracy and the issue of families leaving the city when their children become school age because of worries about the quality of the public schools.

On March 1, 2010, the city administration issued its document, titled "Community Process Generates Somerville's First Vision Statement."

> In Somerville, *We*:
>
> —*Value* the *diversity* of our people, cultures, housing, and economy.
>
> —*Foster* the unique character of our residents, neighborhoods, hills and squares, and the strength of our *community* spirit as expressed in our history, our cultural and social life, and our deep sense of civic engagement.
>
> —*Invest* in the growth of a resilient *economic base* that is centered around transit, generates a wide variety of job opportunities, creates an active daytime population, supports independent local businesses, and secures fiscal self-sufficiency.
>
> —*Promote* a dynamic urban streetscape that embraces public transportation, reduces dependence on the automobile, and is *accessible*, inviting and safe for all pedestrians, bicyclists and transit riders.
>
> —*Build* a *sustainable* future through strong environmental leadership, balanced transportation modes, engaging recreational and community spaces, exceptional schools and educational opportunities, improved community health, varied and affordable housing options, and effective stewardship of our natural resources.
>
> —*Commit* to continued *innovation* and affirm our responsibility to current and future generations in all of our endeavors: business, technology, education, arts, and government. (City of Somerville 2010)

Taken together, these two documents provide not only a vision for this rapidly changing community over the next two decades but also a map of priority issues around which to create shared governance. The two visions—one from a grassroots coalition of civically engaged actors working independently from city government, the other from city government itself (advised by a city-appointed steering committee of local civic leaders, some from the coalition)—have much in common. As I argue in Chapter 6, people I interviewed from three main segments of Somerville's population—older white ethnics, newer immigrants of color, and a newer professional non-immigrant middle class—appear to be largely in agreement on several aspects of their vision for the city's future.

At the same time, there are some clear points of difference in the community versus the city vision statements in terms of points of emphasis, and the degree of specificity between the two documents is at variance. Both address economic development, although the community principles focus directly on creating jobs and keeping the city affordable (naming working-class occupations), while the city document refers more generally to investing in the growth of a resilient economic base. Both allude to the city's diversity of residents and its businesses. Both include environmental issues, such as the importance of green spaces in such a dense urban area, but the community document refers specifically to the need to reduce pollution and toxic substances that affect residents' health. Both address transportation, but the community document specifies the importance of equal access. And, finally, only in the community document is resident participation in community affairs—democratic shared governance, as this paper has termed it—addressed at all. That section of the CCP coalition document reads: "We want to make sure residents are included on an ongoing basis in the planning, design, and zoning changes to the stations and areas around them. . . . We need an easy and clear process for residents to address problems as they come up, with ways of immediately resolving unseen impacts." This suggests the kind of struggle over who runs this city and how they are running it that is the focus of Chapter 7.

Conclusion and Limitations to Shared Governance: Newer Immigrants and Social Citizenship

Large city redevelopment projects are important occasions and opportunities for active engagement because these issues typically affect large numbers of residents from various population segments, involve significant and often controversial investment of community assets, and are characterized by political conflict. In addition to trying to influence governmental decisions about redevelopment, the Somerville voluntary associations that I observed seemed to want to be directly involved in the making of public decisions about redevelopment projects. Much of the established civic and political engagement literature, in contrast, sees voluntary associations as preparing and socializing people for engagement, teaching political skills, and offering spaces for public dialogue that may (or may not) lead to collective political action.[8]

Voluntary associations prominent in Somerville often involve people directly in political action, taking engagement further than what has often been discussed in the literature on civic engagement. My research counters the view of scholars who see voluntary associations as located in some purely "social" sphere, separate from (and averse to) government and politics (Skocpol and Fiorina 1999). This observation contrasts strongly with the views of those who see civic voluntary associations as apolitical and disengaged, perhaps by definition, from efforts to affect public issues (Theiss-Morse and Hibbing 2005: 228).

It is important to point out that relatively small numbers of Somerville's Latino, Brazilian, and Haitian residents are involved in the leadership of the associations I have explored in this chapter. The relative absence of these groups from the leadership of these associations is important evidence in support of my central argument about the absence of social citizenship—full membership and belonging—by Somerville's newer immigrants in the civic and political life of the city. ESNC and the AHOC, both sponsored and staffed by the city's community development agency, do have active newer immigrant members, with a few in leadership positions.[9] However, the MVTF, the STEP, and USN had very few, if any, active members or leaders from the city's immigrant community.

One reason for the relative absence of Latino and Haitian leaders in the MVTF, STEP, and USN seems to be that Latino and Haitian civic leaders have more immediate and pressing local matters of safety and security to deal with—events that require their involvement to protect themselves. I discuss these events and the active engagement they call forth in Chapter 5. To the extent that immigrant engagement is focused on this kind of immediate concern, it provides evidence of their lack of social citizenship. It shows their less than full membership in their own community, which then limits their capacity to take part in mutual governance about broader public issues that go beyond protecting their own safety and security. Their relative absence from the city's public affairs weakens the full potential of civic and political engagement in the city and weakens the capacity that engagement has to strengthen local democracy (Ramakrishnan and Bloemraad 2008a).

Certainly, connections do exist between issues in which immigrant groups are most actively involved and the redevelopment issues that this chapter explores. Other research, for example, has found that law enforcement is a key component of development that causes gentrification and the subsequent displacement of working-class, non-white immigrant populations, who are replaced by middle-class, white professionals. Somerville's Gang Ordinance, discussed in Chapter 5, can be seen as contributing to the displacement of "young brown and black men . . . constructed as dangerous, threatening, in need of surveillance" as part of the "sanitizing racial and class landscape accompanying gentrification" (Perez 2002: 53).

Somerville's immigrant leaders and others are also well aware of how the redevelopment of the major sites discussed here will affect the immigrant population. The creation of a planned whole new retail and residential neighborhood at Assembly Square, major changes being made in Union Square, and the coming of the new subway Green Line all offer opportunities for new immigrants at the same time that these changes threaten them. Indicative of immigrant interest in the city's major development projects, recall that when the CCP coalition held a large community gathering to establish guiding principles for the new subway Green Line, one-third to one-half of the participants appeared to be Latino, Brazilian, or Haitian. The coalition always provided translation in multiple languages, both at their meetings and when the final document was published, suggesting that they expected, planned for, and most importantly, actively sought participation by the city's newer immigrant groups.

When people from the newer immigrant groups were actively involved around redevelopment issues, some through the AHOC and ESNC, their focus tended to be on the issues they saw as affecting them the most: jobs and affordable housing. Active resident Monique Clovet, of Haitian heritage, has occupied a leadership position in one of the associations focused on Assembly Square. She told me: "With the IKEA project, we want East Somerville residents to be the first priority to be hired because, as you know, most of us are immigrant and some of us can't afford to live in East Somerville anymore because the [housing] market is going sky high. So if IKEA moves in . . . it's going to be even higher." As Monique suggested, a pressing concern of Somerville's newer immigrant groups is the threat that these major development projects hold for the loss of affordable housing and the resulting displacement of low-income and working-class residents, many of whom are also among the city's Latinos, Brazilians, and Haitians. That displacement is the focus of Chapter 6.

In Chapter 4, I explore the experiences of old and new immigrant groups in Somerville and suggest a contradiction in how Somerville's identification as an immigrant city both divides and unites these two segments of Somerville's population.

4

Old and New Immigrant Experiences, Today and Yesterday

A collaboration in the fall and winter of 2007 between a Somerville immigrant advocacy organization and Tufts University produced an exhibit called Immigrant City, Then and Now, which was mounted at the local museum. The exhibit and the programs that took place around it sought to provide a space for Somerville's older white ethnic residents and its newer immigrants to acquire a deeper understanding of similarities and differences in their immigrant experiences and to ease some of the tensions between them. A Somerville immigrant advocacy organization called the Welcome Project initiated the exhibit, the same organization whose youth provided language translation at community meetings discussed in Chapter 3. The Welcome Project's mission is to build the collective power of Somerville residents to participate in and shape community decisions (Welcome Project 2011). It was established in 1987 in the city's Mystic Public Housing Development after state-mandated racial integration of the development. During the 1980s, as new residents came from Haiti, Central America, Vietnam, and other parts of the world to join mainly white ethnic residents at the Mystic, tensions grew and tenants and other members of the community founded the Welcome Project to address them. Today, this organization is active in the city in expanding the social citizenship of immigrants and advancing their potential participation in what I have called here mutual shared governance.[1]

Chapter 2 describes the history and demography of groups of immigrants who came to Somerville, both in an earlier era and more recently. These data provide the basis for claims that Somerville can indeed be considered an immigrant city, then and now. This chapter explores what older (mostly second- and third-generation) and newer (mostly first-generation) immigrants have to say about their experiences of living in Somerville.[2] The chapter examines the meaning of these experiences and how they have changed over time, and how they both divide and unify older and newer immigrant groups. I describe how immigrant experiences intersect with class and race, how important it is to learn English, and how racism and anti-immigrant sentiment have co-existed alongside a relatively welcoming environment for immigrants in Somerville in the past and continue to do so today.

The major aim of this chapter is to give voice to what older and newer immigrants have to say about their own experiences. I introduce a concept called the "imaginary" as a lens for some of the core ideas and key beliefs and meanings around these experiences[3] (Strauss 2006). The idea of an "immigrant imaginary" creates a shared experience between two very different groups and supports a sense of shared community. The claimed identity of Somerville as an "immigrant city, then and now," has the potential to create a common history capable of bridging some of the differences (and tensions) between older and newer immigrant generations.

What is missing from this interpretation, from this imaginary, is the fact that the groups that these ideas connect are not only different but also unequal in terms of power, privilege, and access to resources. Many of Somerville's second- and third-generation, white Anglo immigrants have moved into the middle and upper middle class, a few into positions of political power in the city. They typically enjoy the full measure of social citizenship (as well as legal citizenship) that allows them to have their interests represented and eases their participation in local shared governance.

When middle-class residents of Irish and Italian heritage, whose ancestors began coming to the city some 150 years ago, emphasize their immigrant past, they may also be masking their current power and privilege. At the same time that the claim of a shared immigrant heritage connects old and new immigrant groups, it also obscures the reality of more and less privileged race and class positions. Especially relevant in terms of unequal privilege and power, in consideration of this book's focus on civic and political engagement, is the fact that, during the time of my study, residents of Irish and Italian descent who were of immigrant, working-class heritage held virtually all of the elected positions in Somerville government, while Latino, Brazilian, Haitian, and other newer immigrant residents occupied exactly none.

Similar points can be made about the meaning of "working class" and both the positive benefits and negative masking functions of a working-class imaginary. In Chapter 2, I characterize Somerville as still a working-class city in terms of the kinds of jobs most people hold, the kinds of industries that still predominated in the city at the time of my research, and the kinds of jobs that were therefore available in the city. At the same time, many of the second- and third-generation residents who came from working-class backgrounds have long since become college educated and entered decidedly middle-class jobs. This includes the elected officials I spoke with who hold substantial amounts of power in the city, as well as middle-class privilege, but who still identify as working class.[4]

A Working-Class Imaginary That Both Unifies and Divides Different Immigrant Generations

People I talked to from both Somerville's earliest and more recent immigrant groups described a common experience of being low income and working class. Class, in this light, is a potential unifier. As seventy-four-year-old Milos Kosta, a lifelong resident of Greek heritage, put it, with some humor, "My father's idea was that he'd come here, earn a lot of money, buy a lot of land, and have itinerant farmers who would work for him so he wouldn't have to work anymore." Alvarado Marquez, from Central America, started out as a dishwasher, then became a chef, and today has a graduate degree and works as the program director at a local nonprofit. Still, he identifies as working class, explaining that "It's the income. The income I make working in nonprofits is a working-class salary."

Typical of people I talked with from the older group of immigrant-heritage residents who still claim a working-class identity in spite of being college educated and holding professional jobs is Dick O'Neil—grandparents from Ireland, born and raised in Somerville, longtime elected official, holder of an advanced college degree, and owner of his own successful business:[5] "I consider myself working class. . . . Some might say I work in a white-collar profession, and I say, well, you know, I still work. I work with people. It's just that my tools are a keyboard and a wireless phone as opposed to a hammer and nails."

Maria DeCosta, a seventy-six-year-old, lifelong city resident of Italian heritage, with two years of college, who—now retired—previously held administrative jobs, both in the corporate sector and for the city of Somerville, had a similar view: "I think of myself as working class. . . . Working-class people have to go out to work in jobs they can find more than people who are trained. People basically get a job and go to work every day. They don't have this job that pays big bucks; they have regular, average salaries."

When asked if they thought Somerville was still a working-class city or if it had changed, Dick and Maria had somewhat different views, although both emphasized that the city was working class. Dick told me:

> It's definitely still working class. It's just that the collars are a lot more white than blue. . . . They have to work. They have a mortgage. They have kids and responsibilities. It's not like Newton, Wellesley, places like that, where there's [*sic*] people who are independently wealthy and do not have to work, people who have trust funds. . . . Most of the people I talk to [in Somerville] consider themselves working class. They might be professionals, but they're working class.

And Maria, who has lived in East Somerville her whole life, said: "I don't think there is anyone in this city who doesn't have to work, so I consider them working class. Maybe 20 percent of the city is middle class. . . . I think it will always be a working-class city."

Some older residents who were no longer working class in terms of education or occupation appealed to the class position of their immigrant parents to claim what I call a "working-class imaginary." While both Rosemary O'Hanrahan's and Sean Russo's parents had started out at the bottom of the class ladder, Rosemary and Sean both have long since moved up into the middle class. Although this position is admittedly hard won, both are college educated and have held professional jobs their whole lives. Rosemary described her father's job:

> He worked on the assembly line at Ford's [auto plant], and it was a slave job. Later on, they had unions. Mr. Ford was definitely against unions. They could only go to the bathroom at certain times. They used to lay them off for two weeks in the summer, and that was vacation. They got what was good pay for the time, but a lot of the men couldn't stand the pressure of working for the Ford Company. It took its toll. My father died at fifty-eight. He worked twenty-three years for them.

Rosemary also appealed to class to explain why her childhood friends got along despite ethnic and nationality differences: "Poverty. If you're all in the same boat, what's the difference?" Sean, a third-generation resident of Irish and Italian heritage who has lived in the city for nearly sixty years and is a longtime elected city leader, described his family's economic position while he was growing up: "My parents were factory workers. I remember my mother saying to me when my father died, 'You didn't know how poor you were because we all had nothing. We had nothing, but we were all the same.'"

Sean said of his parents:

> They both worked hard. I knew they wanted better for me. I was the first person in my family who went to college. I went to Boston State College. The tuition was over $200 a year. I never applied to places like Boston University, Tufts. There was no way. I felt fortunate that I knew I was getting an education.

When I asked Sean if he thought Somerville was still a working-class city, he said:

> There's two Somervilles now. There's the working-class immigrant city. Then there's the working-class younger people like me who've kind of made it economically and chosen to stay [in the city]. The two don't interact much at all. I have one of those new working-class families next door to me. It consists of multiple residents of Brazilian background, and we don't talk because they don't speak very good English. . . . We don't interact like neighbors.

Angela DeLuca, whose grandparents migrated to Somerville from Italy, has lived her whole life in Somerville and achieved a position of some prominence in the business community. She told me, "We continue to be a blue-collar city. People work; they go home. Whether they are Italian, African American, or Portuguese, they're still hard-working people."

More recent immigrant newcomers to Somerville also sometimes identified as working class, even when objective measures of occupation and education would place them today as middle class. Second-generation black activist Marleine Vera, in her mid-twenties, who came to the area to attend college ten years before and then stayed, said of her family: "We always considered ourselves working class, even though Mom was making a decent amount of money. We were always living from paycheck to paycheck. . . . For our family, it was always a struggle, so that's why I say [we're] working class." When I asked her whether she thought of Somerville as a working-class city, she said, "I do and I feel so much more comfortable in Somerville than I do in Cambridge because people there don't have to struggle and so they can't understand my struggles."

At the same time as immigrants from both older and newer generations expressed a shared working-class and low-income experience, some older residents also recognized that the experience of their parents was different from the experience of today's immigrants in terms of economic opportunity. Rosemary O'Hanrahan offered a clear and compelling understanding of how the shift from an industrial to a service-based economy limits the chances of upward mobility for newer immigrants:

> In bygone days, they might have had staggeringly hard jobs. Now they have long hours, two and three jobs, mostly in service, with low salaries and less of a chance to get ahead. You could get a factory job and eventually make good money and move up the ladder, but if you're in a service job, it's never going to get any better unless you're really unique—and now there are no factory jobs. . . . The open door of manufacturing that led you into the middle class I don't think is there. The only way you're going to get it is [by having] three jobs and saving every penny.

Experiences of Racism: An Acknowledged Difference

Basil Ganas, sixty-four years old and a resident of Somerville since his parents brought him from Greece when he was six years of age, relayed this story about his people's experience:

> I had someone tell me once, "You need to help me [because] we were enslaved all those years; we were under the yolk." I said, "Do you know what I am? . . . The Turks enslaved the Greeks for over seven or eight hundred years. How long were you enslaved? A couple hundred years? And in spite of it all, we were still able to come up under the yolk, maintain our language, maintain our history.

Somewhat in contrast to Basil, a number of older white residents I talked with spontaneously acknowledged their racial-ethnic privilege compared with most newer immigrants of color. When I asked Sean Russo an open-ended question about whether newer immigrants today faced different obstacles than his parents and grandparents, he answered spontaneously in terms of race:

> They're a different color, different customs from what the white immigrants had back then. . . . They're going up against a white establishment. In my generation, it was a white establishment and we

were white, so it wasn't a barrier. It wasn't a barrier to walk into a politician's office and say "I need some help." If I was a Latino walking into that office, it might have been a different reality.

Bruce Riley, a fifty-year resident born and raised in the city and, like Sean, a longtime elected official, also spoke spontaneously about race and racism as differences in earlier versus more recent immigrant experiences:

You hear these stories about "Irish need not apply [for jobs or housing]," but if somebody was walking down the street [then] you wouldn't know if they were Irish or not, so they didn't experience the 24/7 prejudice and discrimination that maybe a black person or a Spanish person would today. . . . There's a lot of prejudice in the world. Somerville's not excluded. . . . Sure, the Irish and the Portuguese and the Italians would never be loved if they sat at the same table, but they just didn't know the difference looking at each other.

Rosemary O'Hanrahan expressed a similar view:

The Irish were discriminated against initially. . . . [T]he difference is you were never hated because of your looks, which today you can be. Today, if you look black or Middle Eastern or Indian, you are different. Earlier, you all looked similar.

Seventy-six-year-old Maria DeCosta, the lifelong city resident of Italian American heritage who was quoted earlier, lives in the eastern part of Somerville, where most of the city's newer immigrants of color also live. She said of her Latino neighbors:

I think it's harder for them. . . . [A]t least my skin was white. They do not have white skin. They have brown skin [and] people are not as willing to bring them into the community. . . . I see it as more difficult for immigrants with a different [skin] color because you know people are more prejudiced about color than they are about white people, no matter what your background.

Andrade Coelho, who is sixty-four and a Portuguese community leader, has lived in Somerville since he was six years old, agreed:

If you look at the immigration experience of Somerville historically, it had been white Caucasian. I grew up [when] the city had probably four or five black families and they all lived on Cameron Avenue, and that was the extent of racial diversity in Somerville. . . . In the 1980s and [19]90s, you see the growth of the Haitian community and it was tough. I remember Haitians being burned out in this town. I remember hearing [about] a Cape Verdean family who bought a house in East Somerville and their children were beaten and ridiculed and they had to sell the house. . . . [Then] the Latino community started to come in, and the Brazilians. Now immigration has color to it, and when I was doing my advocacy work, [I'd hear,] "They're not becoming Americans," and it wasn't that they were immigrants; it was that they were racially different.

Adonia Xanthis, a sixty-six-year-old resident of Greek and Romanian heritage was born and raised in Somerville. She spoke about blacks moving in and described how distressed she was by the racist comments of some of her neighbors:

About fifteen years ago, there were very few black people in Somerville. African Americans, very few. There was this strong African American community in West Somerville, up near [the] Cameron Avenue area. . . . I grew up in that area. Everybody just knew each other. . . . And then, all of a sudden, people started moving in and other people said, "Oh, there's black people coming in" and they were very annoyed. It was like, they're just the same as when the Greeks came in, or when the Italians came in. . . . You know, if they buy a house, it means they're going to take care of it, not let it go to pot.

At the same time, as older white residents spontaneously recognized the racism to which newer immigrants were subjected, older Somervillians also spoke to me about their own painful experiences as immigrants of an earlier era. Maria DeCosta described the harsh ethnic climate for Italians, like herself, who came after the Irish:

Growing up, there were Irish people in the neighborhood; there were English people. The Italians were probably the first invaders . . . because that was what you felt like. After the Italians came the Greeks. After the Greeks, probably Portuguese maybe, but that was way later on. We were the invaders of the neighborhood, and the neighbors were not too happy about it because we were a little different. . . . [W]e didn't belong. . . . I was always a "guinea,"[6] a derogatory term for an Italian . . . so that made me feel inferior. . . . In other words, you were not one of these people. You were an intruder. . . . You know, the bad part is it made me feel ashamed to be who I was because I thought there was something wrong with being Italian. . . . It stayed with me [for] a lot of years.

Yet Maria, like Sean, also noted that all of the early immigrant groups to the city were white: "There was not one black person [who] lived in the neighborhood, not one. In fact, in all of Somerville, there might have been three streets where there were blacks."

Successive ethnic groups, after the Irish and the Italians, formed a status hierarchy, with earlier groups at the top and later ones at the bottom and gradually moving up. Delphia Lekkas, who came to Somerville from Greece in 1953, when she was seven years old, described her experience on arrival: "We came here. We were yelled at by people. The English looked down on the Irish, the Irish looked down on the Italians, and Italians who got into power looked down on the Greeks." Basil Ganas, the sixty-four-year-old resident quoted earlier, like Delphia, was brought to Somerville as a young child. He painted a similar picture: "In the early 1950s [in Somerville], Greeks were a minority that were looked upon by other ethnic groups as the newcomers, the foreigners, the displaced people."

Residents of Greek heritage often identified as not white, and some offered a complex notion of racial categories. Delphia Lekkas, when asked how she identifies in racial-ethnic terms, said, "I identify as Greek, but not white. . . . I was always darker. I remember a racial chant that was directed at me by a few of the neighborhood kids, the n-word. . . . My father was arrested one time because he was Cuban looking. He was dark; he had an accent." Niko Panas also said, "Race-wise, I guess you'd say I'm dark white, not white." Basil Ganas, when asked how he identified in terms of race, understood that race is a historical and changing category: "We more or less evolved into being Caucasian. They tell me I'm no longer a minority." Other scholars have written about how often "becoming American" also meant "becoming white" and how, when they first came to the United States, Italians and Greeks were often seen as non-white (Barrett and Roediger 1997: 6, 8, 9). While no one of Irish heritage whom I talked with mentioned it, even the Irish had their whiteness questioned in the United States during the1840s and 1850s (Barrett and Roediger 1997: 11).

People of color from newer immigrant groups told about the racial hostility they faced. When I asked Alvarado Marquez, who came to Somerville from Central America by himself when he was in his early twenties, what was different about his experience and that of the early immigrants, he said:

> Well, I think it's harder for us, for immigrants who are not white. The immigrants from Ireland, they will make the argument that they were treated badly, and they probably were. But it's easier for them to use the assimilation process. . . . [B]ecause they were white, it was easier for them to get into places. For us, being non-white, it doesn't matter how long you've been here, the color will say you're an immigrant.

Struggles toward Social Citizenship: Learning English, Becoming American, and Preserving One's Own Language and Culture

First-generation immigrants, both old and new, talked about learning English, how it was key to becoming an American, and the challenges of living in both the English-speaking culture and the culture of their home country. This is an experience shared by non-English-speaking immigrants who came to the city fifty or sixty years ago and those who came more recently.

Maria Busconi, born in Somerville in 1938 and raised there by parents who came from Italy, spoke of how language created barriers not only between the early immigrants and "the Americans" but also among different immigrant groups: "Even though the Greeks, Italians, and the Irish lived in the Brickbottom [neighborhood], each [group], because of the language barriers, kept to themselves." Andrade Coelho—Portuguese American, born in the Azores, brought to the United States by his parents at six years of age— has lived in Somerville for over half a century. He came "not knowing a word of English" and was put into kindergarten:

> Back then, there was no bilingual education. It was pretty much a sink-or-swim type of situation. . . . I remember going to school and just sitting there, not knowing what was going on for days, weeks, and months on end. Until you, you begin to catch a little phrase here, a little phrase there. At age six, you're curious, asking questions all the time, you mimic easily, you know. I watched television incessantly, and that's where I learned most of my English. . . . I will admit that, in retrospect, a transitional bilingual education probably

would have helped. . . . I suffered for it later on, especially when I got
up to the high school.

Andrade said, "[I] set my goal to be an American, you know, to lose my
accent," because, like other immigrants who had come to the city before
him, he experienced "a lot of harassment":

> I remember being called a dirty Porgy . . . and if you were an Italian
> kid, you were a dumb wop, and of course, they made fun of the Irish
> kids; they made fun of everybody. But if you had an accent, they
> clearly picked you out . . . [so] I want to be mainstream, to be like
> everybody else. I worked really hard on losing my accent, and you
> know the only difficulty, I was sort of living in two worlds, because
> at home we spoke nothing but Portuguese. . . . I was still very culture
> bound to being Portuguese, had to speak the language, the foods,
> the church, the festivals, the celebrations. But my family also cel-
> ebrated Thanksgiving, [and] we celebrated the Fourth of July, so
> you're American and you're this too.

Basil Ganas told a similar story about the impact of losing his accent:

> I was considered a "Greece ball." Some of my best friends continued
> that stereotype. I was at the bottom of the totem pole back in the fif-
> ties. I grew out of it by being able to speak perfectly so you couldn't
> tell whether I was Greek, Italian, or Irish. Those were the ethnic
> groups then, the major ones. My father felt very hurt, degraded, and
> demeaned by the Irish community. At that time, the Irish were the
> cat's meow, and the Greeks were the grease balls. We were the His-
> panics of today.

Andrea Ferro, whose parents migrated to Somerville from the Azores in 1951,
was born and raised in Somerville, although she still speaks Portuguese at
home. She told me how her parents' limited English shaped her school years:

> We lived next door to a Greek family. They were the people I identi-
> fied with. They were like us. They spoke another language, and they
> ate different food and went to a different church, just like I did. . . .
> My biggest thing is that my parents weren't involved at all in my edu-
> cation because they didn't speak English.

When I asked Andrea how she thought the experiences of more recent immigrants were similar to and different from those of earlier immigrants, such as her parents, she talked about learning English:

> People don't understand that, when you want a child to learn a language immediately, [and you] put a kid from Brazil and a kid from Haiti who don't speak English in a regular classroom . . . that it would be better to have these children in their own classroom, where they could learn English along with their own language, and then gradually, as they do learn English . . . put them into the regular classroom with all the other children.

Newer immigrants also pointed to the importance of language. Juliana Silva came to the United States by herself from Brazil as a young adult in 1992. She described still being marginalized today because of her accent: "I do feel, because of my accent and everything, I'm not quite considering this home." Vitor Branco, who came to the United States from Brazil in 1980, when he was in eighteen years old, and moved to Somerville in 1988, said that having to learn English was a main reason why he moved from a different Massachusetts city with a larger and (in his view) more insulated Brazilian population: "I said, if I stay with the Brazilian people, I would never learn English. . . . That's why I moved to Somerville, because it was a new place that forced me to speak English rather than Portuguese."

Even though having to speak English was important enough to Vitor that he moved from one town to another, he still, like many later, more contemporary generations of immigrants, wants himself and his children to retain his first language: "I had a big lesson when I took my first daughter back to Brazil to introduce her to her grandma. She was asking Grandma for a glass of water and Grandma could not respond because she did not understand. That was my big lesson that I should teach my kids Portuguese at home and they will learn English at school."

Young leader Ramon Vazquez, born and raised in Somerville, felt similarity, saying, "You learn English, okay, no problem—but at the same time, there are some things you want to hold on to. There is no official language in the United States."

People from the younger immigrant generation also objected to people who tried to limit the use of any language besides English. Isabel Garcia, who has lived in the city for nearly twenty years, having moved there at age twenty, said:

You hear a lot of people that are like, "If you don't know English, get them [*sic*] out." They hear us talking in Spanish because it's considered rude if your friend speaks Spanish to you and you don't speak back in Spanish to her. They say, "Speak in English," and you are looking at them like "Why? We are not speaking about you. It's just a conversation." When Haitians . . . are speaking their language, we [Latinos] don't say, "Hey, speak English." Everybody should be learning a little more cultural stuff.

Vitor's, Ramon's, and Isabel's ideas about retaining their original language even as they became facile with English is consistent with the thinking of scholars who reject what has historically been the U.S. dominant model of assimilation. In this older model, immigrant groups are asked to give up their original language as a requirement of social citizenship. Indeed, in today's global, transnational economy, retaining these multi-lingual and cross-cultural qualities may provide economic advantages for newer immigrants (Glenn 2000: 12).

Isabel also shared her frustration with how language poses a barrier to jobs and social acceptance, even for professionals who are highly educated:

I've seen my friends, lawyers and whatnot, unable to practice here, college professors not able to teach here. They come and get all their paperwork, and it's not enough. Give these people the test in their language and you see what you are missing out on. . . . Like if they need to pass the bar exams, give them that exam in Spanish. I'm sure there are lot of Hispanics who need lawyers, legal aides.

Everyone I talked with across generations shared Isabel's understanding that learning English was essential for accessing economic opportunities, even for highly educated immigrants. Rosario Gonzales was in school for an advanced professional degree in her country of origin when she first came to the United States. When she arrived here, she worked at a low-level job at Dunkin' Donuts because she did not speak English:

The owner was Greek. . . . One time, one of the workers didn't come in and I was washing the dishes and serving the customers. I had learned the names of the doughnuts [in English]. It was easy, you know. So I started serving the customers, and my boss . . . called me in and said, "No more washing dishes. Tomorrow you serve the customers." So, from then on, I was on my way up.

An Immigrant Imaginary: Bridging Generations and Nationalities?

For the most part, both older and newer generations I talked with see Somerville as a city whose history and tradition has been to welcome new immigrants. In this sense, what I am calling the city's immigrant imaginary is a bridging concept that builds community. Andrea Ferro said, "I'm proud of Somerville describing itself as an immigrant city. The mayor comes from an immigrant family, just as I do, and he's bilingual [like I am]." Adonia Xanthis said about growing up in the city, "There were a lot of Greeks, a lot of Italian and Irish immigrants. And everybody got along well because everybody was an immigrant." Adonia described how, during the 1990s, she saw new black immigrants moving into the neighborhood where she grew up: "It was . . . like when the Greeks came or the Italians came, people [were] coming in looking to better their lives."

Older white Anglo Somerville residents often cited their own immigrant backgrounds as a factor in their support for this relatively welcoming climate. Because all of the respondents in this study were actively engaged in some way in their community, with many of them genuine leaders, they may not be typical of city residents who are not as engaged. Maria DeCosta, a seventy-six-year-old lifelong resident of Italian American heritage who is still involved in community affairs, said:

> There are some that you know just will never accept it, [but] if you were part of the immigrant persona at one time [then] you were more welcoming to other people. . . . Some longtime city residents don't like it. . . , They feel as though immigrants are lower-class people. . . . [They look at] the immigrants at Foss Park and [ask] why [they are] hanging out there . . . but I feel as though they have a right to be there and [to be] looking for work and they're not hurting anyone, so what's the difference. . . . People feel as though the immigrants are taking something away from them, but they're not. You know, there is misinformation.

Adapting to a new culture requires managing multiple identities and managing one's sense of feeling at home. As Juliana Silva told me, "When I go to Brazil, I still say it's home. After twenty years now, I still don't have the sense [Somerville] is home." Even though Marleine Vera was born in the United States, she told me she still identified with the immigrant experience of her parents and what they went through: "Growing up, I constantly felt

I was in a different culture and trying to help my parents navigate it. . . . I had to explain to my younger siblings, 'This is how you apply to college'— and with my mom, if she had problems at work, I would say, 'Well, if you think about it this way, you can understand why the other person said that.'" When I asked Marleine what she saw as similarities and differences between her experience and that of her parents, she pointed to how "the second generation [like me] becomes the connector," along with the challenge of managing multiple identities: "I've always struggled with where I belong because my identity is not fully American."

Unlike Marleine, who was born in the United States, and unlike Juliana, who is also relatively younger and has been in the United States for a shorter time, Vitor Branco (a Brazilian American who has been in the United States for nearly thirty years, since age eighteen) said, "I feel this is my home. I'm settled here and I really love it. I feel like an American." Vitor offered advice for immigrants who were having trouble adapting:

> I know friends [who] feel like they are being discriminated against, and I keep telling them, 'Listen, you have to change yourself because now you are in a different country.' You have to learn how they work the system, and that is what many Brazilians don't do because they are so busy working and they don't pay attention to what's around them. They don't really bother learning the system because they are here temporarily for the kids. I am here permanently.

Somerville residents whose experiences were much distant from those of Marleine and Vitor, that is, whose families had been there for several generations, often still identified with the immigrant experience. Dick O'Neil told me that Somerville today is "still very much an immigrant city" and said, "We are really the classic melting pot, [both] now and back then, when it was Irish, Italian, and Portuguese."

Rosemary O'Hanrahan, a lifetime resident in her mid-seventies, offered an insightful analysis about why Somervillians hold to a common immigrant identity rather than to, as she said, "one nationality" that excludes other groups. She contrasted Somerville with neighborhoods in Boston that have been historically singularly identified with her own racial-ethnic group, white ethnic Irish. While she diplomatically did not name these neighborhoods, both Charlestown and South Boston have been known in the past as ethnic enclaves that were hostile to people they saw as outsiders. "Somerville," she said," has never been a one-nationality immigrant city. We've always been an immigrant city, but not just one [nationality]. That's part of Somerville's uniqueness, I think." Thirty-year resident and activist Sam Martin had a similar view: "Somerville seems to have a bit of everybody [—unlike other local towns, such as] Lawrence, which is largely Hispanic. New Bedford is Brazilian. Lowell is Cambodian-Khmer."

While this diversity among the immigrant population carries the possibility of a shared immigrant identity across racial-ethnic differences, it also creates a major challenge in bringing a community of immigrants to act together politically, especially in terms of electing new people to office. I discuss this further in Chapter 7.

Anti-immigrant Hostility and Displacement of an Immigrant Working Class

While people I talked with agreed that Somerville is relatively welcoming to new immigrants, racist and anti-immigrant acts do occur. They pose a serious barrier to the shared social citizenship necessary for participation in shared local governance. Although everyone I talked with said that the city's immigrant climate had improved over the years, these acts create ongoing conflict and tension among Somerville's diverse population. They also pose a threat to Somerville's claim of being an immigrant city, a claim that people across its different segments told me they want to keep as a valued tradition and vision for the future. I consider this shared vision further in Chapter 6.

Ramon Vazquez, a rising young leader in his mid-thirties, was born in Somerville of immigrant parents and is a product of the Somerville public schools. Ramon had awful stories to tell about his experience growing up in the city in the early 1990s—and, like most of those I talked with, he shared an impression of how much better things are now:

> My sisters and I were the only minorities in the [elementary] school, and the school system wasn't prepared for what was happening with me. So, a lot of times, my father would have to come and advocate on my behalf for my right to have an education without having to fight every day. . . . When I was growing up, it was practically the norm being called "spic." I mean it was practically my middle name. I remember having windows smashed with bricks saying "get outta here" and that kind of stuff. It was a rough time. . . . It's changed 100 percent. . . . When I was younger, there was a lot of racism. You still hear it, but it's a whole lot less than before.

Rosario Gonzales, who moved to Somerville at that same time, in 1991, told me: "When I bought my house . . . my next door neighbor move out [*sic*]. She sold her house because she didn't want to be next to us. . . . She told us . . . [b]ecause you are Latino and I don't want you in my neighborhood."

When I asked Juliana Silva how her relationship with second- and third-generation, white ethnic residents in the city had changed in the fifteen years since she came to the city, she said: "It has not changed. It has not changed. You get to talk to people, but the old Italians and Irish, you cannot get to them." Juliana, who holds a position of some authority, related to me the following story as a dramatic example of being made to feel like an outsider:

> I've called the police two times already [this year]. . . . They call my house. They said to me, "You bunch of immigrants, what are you doing here?" And every single year, [my staff] calls me and says, "You need to come here [to the office]," and it's always around race. I went and one said, "I thought I was getting the supervisor." Guess what, I'm it. Most likely, it's old-time Somervillians. It was very hard, very painful. . . . It's just people who don't know better, who don't know how not to judge people by where you come from.

Alvarado Marquez, a Somerville resident for nearly thirty years, described an incident that happened to him:

> One time, we were having this meeting with the chief of police at the police station, and I was walking in[to] the station and a couple of police officers were coming out. I think they thought I didn't understand English . . . and I hear them say, "Here's trouble." . . . Here we are, trying to work with the police, and I'm walking in and these police officers look at me and say, "Here's trouble."

Monique Clovet came to the United States from Haiti in the 1970s, moved to Somerville in 2000, and bought a two-family home. She described a hostile welcome: "You don't find too many black people here ten years ago. I parked my car on [my] street and someone gave me four flat tires. That's the first thing that happened in Somerville. It wasn't a nice place. I was dealing with racism." Vertus Bernique, a black Haitian community leader who came to Somerville in 1989, when he was twenty-nine years old, told me:

> When I came here, there was basically nobody to talk to and I was lost in knowing what to do. I rented an apartment and there was no

heat, and I didn't know who to call, so it was cold and we spent a week in a house with no heat, and my daughter at that time was two years old. . . . When I first moved here, [older whites] saw a group different from themselves . . . and basically there was a lot of fear.

A few of the older white ethnic immigrants I talked with expressed the anti-immigrant attitudes that Alvarado and Juliana and others had experienced. Maria Busconi, when asked what she saw as some of the problems in the city today, said that new immigrant groups are "using up resources. I hear they're on the public dole. When most of the immigrants came in the early 1900s, there was no public dole. They were just left to themselves." When asked how she thought immigrants today and those who came earlier were similar and different, Delphia Lekkas, who came to Somerville from Greece as a child in the 1950s, had this to say: "My father had the good sense to buy his own medical insurance. Today it isn't like that. Everything is just handed. That's why I think people today are so angry with immigrants, illegal immigrants."

Adonia Xanthis, a retired teacher who taught her students (and her neighbors) to be more accepting of black and other new immigrants in the 1980s, nonetheless struggled with her own feelings about undocumented immigrants: "Immigration is a lot different now, where we have so many illegal immigrants . . . although you feel for them too. I mean, they want an opportunity. That's why they're here. That's why everybody came here, for an opportunity. So it's very hard."

In contrast to Delphia and Adonia, Andrea Ferro, who was born and raised in Somerville after her parents came from Portugal's Azores in the early 1950s, was concerned about the injustice of a growing anti-immigrant sentiment in the United States:

> I think the immigrant today, there's a stigma. . . . Resources are tight and there's a growing intolerance. There's not a feeling that we're all in this together. I feel really bad about that because I think that most immigrants want to come to this country for the same reasons our parents came to this country. . . . To me, it's escalating. It's all over the country, and it's getting worse. For immigrants, it's very difficult.

For the most part, both newer and older Somerville immigrants I talked with saw Somerville as having become more open and welcoming over time. Alvarado Marquez said:

It was worse in the 1980s. There were all these issues happening. . . .
A lot of us have been working actively in making people understand
who we are and what we are doing here. . . . I think that the Somervillians are becoming more open minded . . . not completely, but
more than they used to be in the 1980s. I also think that the community in Somerville has changed. A lot of these older residents moved
or died, so it's a new wave of middle-class people moving into Somerville. A lot of them, not all of them, but a lot of them, are more open
minded and receptive to who's here because they are being attacked
too [for being] yuppies.

Haitian activist Vertus Bernique saw more changes than Alvardo noted, and
he too attributed these changes to activism by immigrants themselves:

I've seen a lot of change in Somerville. There's been a lot of struggle,
a lot of fights, a lot of misperception. . . . When I first moved here [in
1989, people here] saw a group of people different from themselves
in many ways, the white community, and basically, there was a lot of
fear. . . . I think [then] that many people got involved, many people,
and tried to create more communication, more education. So this
basic idea of the fear that many white Somervillians had has mostly
disappeared because there have been so many efforts by whites, Haitians, Latinos to involve people in dialogue. . . . When people come
together and talk . . . we get to know each other, through social dialogue, and we need to have more of that.

Monique Clovet, who was welcomed to the city a decade ago by having her
tires slashed, said:

Now I love it . . . [a]lthough you still have some people that don't
deal [well] with what's happening; they don't want to deal with it. It
still exists, but it's changed for all of us—Latinos, Brazilians, Portuguese, Italians, Haitians, Africans—because you can see the diversity
now. It's more acceptable, and people start to get used to people, no
matter what background or culture you do have. They start to adjust.
They are more tolerant now than ten years ago.

Juliana Silva, who had the frightening experience of being telephoned at
home by anti-immigrant callers, felt the contrast of a more positive atti-

tude toward new immigrants from newer Somerville residents: "I feel the resistance from longtime Somerville residents, a sense of ownership. . . . I don't feel the same with the younger newcomers. We get along more. We have a different approach." Adonia Xanthis talked about how, as a teacher at Somerville High School, she said to students who expressed immigrant prejudice: "There would always be a couple of kids who would say, 'Oh, we don't want those stupid,' then they'd name an ethnic group, and I'd say, 'You know, we are all foreigners; we all came from someplace. If it wasn't you, it was your mother, and if it wasn't your mother, it was your grandmother.'" Adonia also expressed her irritation with adults who were not accepting of new immigrants: "I see discrimination. Some of it is very subtle. . . . I remember a conversation . . . and someone said, 'Well, I don't go to Market Basket in Somerville because it's all foreigners.' I mean . . . who cares who's in the market, and plus you were a foreigner too. I mean like this was an adult."

The importance of expanding full community membership (social citizenship) and participation (shared governance) to the city's newer immigrants was expressed by Andrade Coelho, who, like a number of both older and newer immigrants, is proud of Somerville's working-class immigrant history. He worries that the city has become out of reach economically for newer immigrants and offered a complex view of class and race relationships and the future of Somerville:

> [The city] is changing, and as it gentrifies more and more . . . people think you have less chance of racism, but I think in time, you have a greater chance of it. Because what you do is begin to stratify economically, and when you stratify economically, you only have to look around to see who's got most of the money, and they continue to be white. . . . Unless the city develops a plan [to] keep diversity in the city, economics eventually are just gonna win—and [then] where do the immigrants go?

The city's community development agency, the Somerville Community Corporation (SCC) has drawn on the potential of class-based resident displacement as a way of bringing together different generations of immigrant-identified residents. Through the voluntary associations that the SCC supports—East Somerville Neighbors for Change and the Affordable Housing Organizing Committee—SCC has had some success in bringing together a racially and ethnically diverse group of working-class residents focused on preserving affordable housing. The potential to extend social citizenship for newer immigrants and then to increase their active participation (in shared governance) more generally remains to be seen. Chapter 5 deals with when and how newer immigrants in the city have become actively engaged in recent decades around urgent local issues that threaten their immediate safety and security.

5

Immigrant Civic
and Political Engagement

This chapter examines three key events in Somerville in recent years that called out organized civic and political engagement by immigrant residents and their advocates and allies. All three events threatened immigrant safety and security. To the extent that engagement is limited to this kind of occasion, I argue that the city's immigrants are restricted in their participation in public affairs. I base this argument in the view that, when people have access to the benefits of social citizenship, they are "able to act . . . for the common good, rather than out of [their own] . . . immediate needs" (Glenn 2000: 7).[1]

I locate the participation, or lack of participation, of immigrants in community affairs within a larger framework of a struggle over social citizenship. As I have explained, social citizenship is not simply a legal status. It refers rather to an invitation to full participation, membership, and a sense of belonging to a community (Bloemraad 2006: 1; Glenn 2011: 3; Marshall 1964). Social citizenship is, then, about inclusion and exclusion. For example, while U.S. non-citizens are excluded from the right to vote and from military service, they are (theoretically) included in basic civil rights, such as freedom of speech and due process, and social entitlements, such as access to public education (Glenn 2000: 12). Citizenship, in this sense, is a socially constructed category "continually transformed through political struggle" (Glenn 2000: 3).

Research about U.S. immigrants has, until very recently, had little to say about civic and political engagement. The incorporation of immigrants into public and community life has been largely neglected in favor of studies of social mobility and assimilation (Ramakrishnan and Bloemraad 2008a: 9). Local contexts are an especially important (and understudied) area for understanding immigrant incorporation because, while federal immigration policy determines who may enter the United States, it leaves to local actors all of the issues that arise when immigrants actually come to live in host communities (Farris 2003: 5; Light 2006). While some local U.S. communities have established policies to exclude immigrants from civic and political participation (Varsanyi 2010), urban locales sometimes institute policies and practices explicitly aimed at including newer immigrants and their concerns in community affairs (Ramakrishnan and Bloemraad 2008a: 24; Wells 2004). A few cities have even extended to non-citizens the right to vote in local elections.[2] Chicago, for example, has for many years allowed non-citizen residents to vote for members of the school board. Before exploring immigrant participation in Somerville, I provide some national and Massachusetts state-level context.

The United States today is deeply polarized on the issue of immigration, and immigrants to this country are far less likely to become legal citizens compared with nations such as Canada. In 2001, for example, only 40 percent of U.S. foreign-born residents were legal citizens compared with 72 percent in Canada (Bloemraad 2006: 2). In Massachusetts, of nearly 300,000 legal immigrants eligible for citizenship, only 10 percent claimed citizenship in 2008 (Sacchetti 2009b).

The main reason for this discrepancy between the United States and Canada appears to be how differently these two nations receive immigrant residents (Bloemraad 2006). In recent decades, U.S. immigration policy has been concerned mainly with border control and placing strict limits on who is allowed into the country. U.S. policy neither encourages nor supports immigrants to pursue legal citizenship. Canada, in contrast, is guided by a policy of multi-culturalism that urges immigrants to become citizens and assists them in so doing. It allows immigrant residents to retain dual citizenship, has a three-year residency requirement (versus five in the United States), and provides various government supports, such as funding English classes and providing job search assistance (Bloemraad 2006).[3]

These two nations, similar in many ways, offer useful examples of contrasting sides in the debate articulated in Chapter 1. Should receiving nations act affirmatively to incorporate immigrants into both legal and social citizenship, as Canada does? Or is it sufficient, as in the United States, to simply offer immigrants who decide on their own to seek legal citizenship the same rights as citizens?

To apply for U.S. citizenship, immigrants must be permanent residents for at least five years, or three years if married to a U.S. citizen. Once the application process is complete, in Massachusetts, it takes, on average, less than four months to obtain citizenship, much less than the national average (Sacchetti 2009b). The process includes payment of a $656 fee, which has increased ten times in the past two decades and which is the highest among Western nations (Sacchetti 2009b). Applicants must also complete a form, get fingerprinted, be interviewed in English, and pass a test in English on U.S. history and civics. Finding a way to learn English is difficult because more than 150,000 people in Massachusetts are on waiting lists for English classes (Sacchetti 2009b).

Undocumented immigrants, called "illegal aliens" under U.S. law, are a main target for anti-immigrant sentiment, although people who come legally to the United States from other countries are also profoundly affected. According to independent estimates by the Pew Hispanic Center, about 11.1 million undocumented immigrants lived in the United States in 2009, a decline from 12 million in 2007 (Preston 2010c). About three-fourths of undocumented immigrants are, to use the U.S. Census term, Hispanic (Preston 2010c). Latinos—whether U.S. citizens, legal non-citizens, or undocumented—all suffer from the hostility directed toward those who are here illegally. A 2010 Pew survey found that nearly two-thirds of Latinos said that discrimination was a major problem for them. This is an increase from just over one-half in 2007. Latinos who were surveyed attributed increased discrimination to an increase in U.S. hostility toward illegal immigration (Preston 2010b).

Pew estimates that 14 percent of Massachusetts residents are immigrants (912,310 people), and of these about 20 percent (190,000) are undocumented (Aizenman 2009). I use this 20 percent figure in Chapter 2 to estimate that about five thousand undocumented immigrants may be living in Somerville today. Immigrants become undocumented ("illegal") in several ways besides entering the United States surreptitiously. These include remaining in the United States beyond their allotted time when holding a student or employment visa or through temporary refugee status.

The U.S. Immigrant Reform and Control Act (IRCA) was passed in 1986 to prevent employers from hiring those who enter the United States illegally and signaled the beginning of a new wave of anti-immigrant sentiment (Wells 2004: 1308). This sentiment intensified in the 1990s, and other national and local policies were passed to prevent immigrants from coming to the United States and to curtail their circumstances if they did come

(Varsanyi 2010). Immigrants today are blamed for taking American jobs, depleting social welfare coffers, and elevating crime rates, along with a range of other pressing problems in the United States (Wells 2004: 1309). A growing number of cities and states are passing anti-immigrant laws like those that the *New York Times* labeled "cruel, racist, and counterproductive" in a 2011 Independence Day editorial ("It Gets Even Worse" 2011).

U.S. federal, state, and local laws have erected barriers to higher education and housing to undocumented immigrants and their children. While a 1982 U.S. Supreme Court decision guarantees that undocumented students receive a K–12 public school education, a 1996 federal law bars them from receiving benefits toward a college degree, such as financial aid. Forty states require them to pay out-of-state tuition rates (Sacchetti 2010a).[4] While state-supported public housing in Massachusetts, as directed by a 1977 federal court ruling, does not require proof of legal citizenship, local authorities require that only documented immigrants be allowed to reside there (Harmon 2010). A 2010 survey by a Boston law school found seven to one support among Massachusetts voters for state housing requiring proof of legal residency (Harmon 2010).

At the federal level, the election of President Barack Obama in November 2008 seemed to set a new course for dealing with immigration compared with the anti-immigrant policies of President George W. Bush. Obama campaigned on a promise to make immigration reform a top priority, and Latino immigrants voted for him in large numbers (78 percent), based on that promise (Sacchetti 2008c). On the positive side, in November 2009, U.S. Homeland Security Secretary Janet Napolitano halted a series of proposed immigration raids and announced a change in policy (Hsu 2009). She also said that the Obama administration would insist on measures to provide a path to citizenship for undocumented immigrants nationwide. However, immigrant advocates have been disappointed that the Obama administration deported a record number of 400,000 immigrants in 2009 and then again in 2010 (Preston 2011). And while sentiment may be growing for immigration reform (Sacchetti 2008d), Obama himself has said he sees no "shortcuts" to help illegal immigrants (Preston 2011).

At the state level, early in 2007, the newly elected governor of Massachusetts, Deval Patrick, rejected an agreement by former governor Mitt Romney to assign thirty state troopers to help enforce federal immigration law (Sacchetti 2010b). In the fall of 2008, Patrick launched a statewide New Americans Initiative to gather recommendations about how to better incorporate new immigrants (Sacchetti 2008b, 2010b). Patrick endorsed the report's recommendations and committed to implementing them during 2009, including giving in-state tuition rates to immigrant students (the topic of a major campaign by local immigrant advocacy groups) (Sacchetti 2009d), ensuring translation at state public meetings, and funding citizenship programs (Sacchetti 2010b).

Several Massachusetts cities and towns joined Somerville in pledging that their local police departments would not take it upon themselves to enforce federal immigration laws. I heard this pledge repeated several times by city aldermen at Somerville public meetings (including aldermen who did not support other immigrant-friendly measures considered later, such as the Welcoming Somerville initiative). Somerville police argued, as did other police departments nationally (Wells 2004: 1325), that the practice would inspire distrust among immigrants, thus discouraging them from reporting criminal activity, and that it would divert police from pursuing more serious crime (Sacchetti 2009a).

During his 2006 campaign and into 2010, Governor Patrick had also endorsed the policy of allowing illegal immigrants to obtain driver's licenses. Somerville's police chief at the time also publicly supported this policy (Sacchetti 2009e, 2010c).[5] The state of Massachusetts, like the nation, seemed to be on a new and different track in terms of measures to better incorporate immigrants (even undocumented ones) into the public life of their communities and society.

As these and other events seemed to advance the cause of immigrants during the period of my research, anti-immigrant forces were mobilizing and the backlash had its effect. By 2008, the U.S. Census reported a decline in the numbers of Latino and other immigrants (legal and illegal) coming to the United States, largely because of the faltering economy and loss of jobs. However, some areas, such as greater Boston, continued to show gains (Ohlemacher 2008a, 2008b; Yen 2009). By the summer of 2010, the Obama administration's prospects for Congressional support looked dim in light of pressing concerns about jobs and the economy caused by the major recession that began in the fall of 2008 (Hsu 2010). Negative reaction to Governor Patrick's 2009 initiative was swift, with critics accusing him of failing to make it clear whether his support for immigrants included those who were undocumented. By the time he began his campaign for reelection in 2010, Patrick was less outspoken about his plans for immigration reform (Sacchetti 2010b). Although he denied having changed his position, Patrick had accomplished little in terms of actual reform as he faced a tough campaign for reelection.

An indication of what Patrick had to contend with during his run for reelection occurred on May 27, 2010, when the Massachusetts state Senate passed a sweeping piece of legislation that, if made into law, would bar the state's estimated more than 180,000 undocumented immigrants from public health care, housing, and higher education benefits. It would also have created an anonymous hotline to report illegal immigrants. A Massachusetts state representative from Somerville told the *New York Times* that "her office was inundated with hostile calls after she voted against a similar proposed law in April" (Goodnough 2010). While the law reportedly had little chance of eventual passage, reports suggested that it "dramatically changed the state's image as a compassionate, immigrant-friendly state" (Bierman and Sacchetti 2010). Among the immigrant advocacy organizations that mobilized immediately to counteract the proposed bill was Somerville's Centro Presente, which was highlighted in local media reports.

In addition to the proposed anti-immigrant legislation, another vivid example of what Governor Deval Patrick was up against appeared in the area's conservative *Boston Herald* on the morning of July 21, 2010. A huge headline screamed, "Thanks to Deval, FREEBIES FOR ILLEGALS." The article attacked undocumented immigrants for getting a "free ride" on taxpayer-funded state services (Chabot 2010). In contrast, *The Boston Globe* had earlier reported, "Immigrants pour billions of dollars into state coffers every day in taxes" (quoted in Sacchetti 2009c).

In spite of attacks on his liberal immigration stance, Deval Patrick emerged victorious, with a sizable margin in what Boston's major newspaper called a "brutalizing campaign" to be reelected governor of Massachusetts (Sacchetti 2010c). He immediately issued a statement noting his intention to focus on "pushing for changes for legal and illegal immigrants alike," returning to implementing the recommendations of his 2008-initiated New Americans Initiative, aimed at better incorporating new immigrants (Sacchetti 2010b).

In light of the governor's past support and then recommitment to support for immigrants, local immigrant advocates were stunned when unnamed Massachusetts state officials announced just a month later, in December 2010, their intention to join the federal Secure Communities program (Sacchetti 2010d). Secure Communities "allows local law enforcement to check the immigration status of every person, including U.S. citizens, who are booked into a county or local jail" (Preston 2010a). The U.S. Office of Homeland Security reported that deportations in 2009 reached a record high as a result of the new Secure Communities program (Preston 2010a). The program is in pilot status until 2013, and the federal government has announced plans to make it mandatory. There are fifty-one legal grounds on which non-citizens (illegal *or legal*) may be deported, in four categories: criminal, immigration (e.g., smuggling, fraud), immigration status, and security (e.g., espionage, genocide, terrorist acts) (Tooby 2005). Undocumented people may be deported on arrest. Conviction is not required for deportation (Massachusetts Immigrant and Refugee Advocacy Coalition 2005).

In June 2011, Governor Patrick responded to protests and teach-ins by local immigrant organizations by joining the states of New York and Illinois in withdrawing from participation in Secure Communities. Somerville immigrant organization Centro Presente was the lead organization in the efforts of Massachusetts against this program. With a growing number of local governments and states now wanting to opt out, the Obama administration says that it is working to improve Secure Communities, a claim a June 2011 *New York Times* editorial called "Too Little, Too Late."

Of the 195,722 immigrants deported nationally through the Secure Communities program in 2009 alone, one-half had never been convicted of any crime. Federal immigration authorities blocked researchers from obtaining further information about these nearly 100,000 deported immigrants (Preston 2010a). A 2010 *New York Times* editorial stated, "The Obama administration insists that [this program's] primary focus is on catching and deporting the worst, most dangerous offenders. But its record shows otherwise. It has been using its powers to detain and deport tens of thousands of immigrants who have no criminal records and pose no conceivable danger to their communities" ("Confusion over Secure Communities" 2010). A 2010 *Boston Globe* editorial expressed similar concern about "evidence that Secure Communities has been sweeping up minor offenders along with dangerous felons" ("Using Police on Immigration" 2010).

Both an Official Welcome for Newer Immigrants and a Local Struggle over Social Citizenship

Among immigrant leaders interviewed for this study, some were, at the time I spoke with them, or had been city government appointees in departments aimed at serving the interests of immigrant groups, such as the Human Rights Commission and the Multi-cultural Commission (no longer active). A few have run unsuccessfully for Somerville public office. Several are founders and/or past or current directors of organizations and associations that, in addition to being actively involved in local public affairs, represent the views, interests, and concerns of their constituents to local government officials and assist new immigrants to adapt to their new environments and integrate into their new communities (De Graauw 2008; de Leon et al. 2009: 9; Farris 2003; Hung 2007). These local immigrant organizations provide services to newer immigrants, advocate on their behalf, and promote immigrant civic and political engagement (Le Roux 2007). They train immigrants to be leaders in their own communities, educate them about the U.S. and local political systems, hold forums on local and national political issues, host local candidates' nights, offer language and citizenship classes, and urge immigrants to eventually take part in the electoral process (de Leon et al. 2009: 32).

The city of Somerville is officially welcoming for immigrants, as I describe briefly in Chapter 1. During the 1980s, it was one of only twenty cities in the United States that passed a sanctuary resolution (Wells 2004: 1319). This meant that, in 1987, Somerville declared itself a "city of refuge" for new immigrants, mandating that city employees need not give information to federal immigration officials on residents' status, and guaranteeing city services (including public schooling) to immigrants, regardless of whether their status was documented or undocumented (Bennett 1993; Wells 2004: 1318, 1319). Alberto Dias, who fled almost certain death in Central America to migrate illegally to Somerville during the 1980s, and who has since become a U.S. citizen, told me, "Cambridge and Somerville became a sanctuary for refugees, and a lot of people from my country came to Somerville." His experience offers an example of a local community choosing to extend some measure of social citizenship to new immigrants, regardless of their legal status.

Six years later, however, Somerville succumbed to national and local anti-immigrant pressure and backed away from the sanctuary resolution, claiming that new immigrants who were flocking to the city were draining city services and crowding schools. In 1993, the city's Board of Aldermen formally rescinded that resolution and replaced it with a weaker affirmation, stating simply that it had "historically welcomed newcomers" (Bennett 1993).

By the summer of 2007, Somerville immigrant advocates sought to reinstate the original, more strongly worded Sanctuary City resolution. They abandoned that effort when it became clear that most of the city's aldermen would not vote to restore it. Alderman Sean Russo, a lifetime Somerville resident, told me at the time, "I was at the barber shop this morning, the white barber shop. All the . . . older people said to me, 'Boy, you better not vote for that [new] Sanctuary City resolution.'" Russo admitted his own ambivalence:

> The mayor has been out front saying he supports immigrant participation in the city, that we're not going to deny them education, human services, police services, and so forth because of their status, either legal or illegal. There are members of the Board [of Aldermen]

I know who feel strongly that we should not be giving city services to people not here legally—and I am frankly torn.

In the summer of 2008, several local immigrant service and advocacy organizations joined to advance what they thought would be a more acceptable alternative, a pledge card campaign called Welcoming Somerville. They planned to ask elected city officials and members of the general public to sign a card, stating in part, "I commit to publicly reject the politics of division and isolation that fan anger and hate against any person or community and to work toward just, workable, and humane immigration policies that are anchored in America's finest ideals and core values." The back of the card said, "The current anti-immigrant rhetoric fails to recognize the economic and cultural contributions that immigrants make to our Commonwealth." It listed seven beliefs that signatories subscribe to, including one stating that "harsh immigration enforcement policies violate civil and human rights of immigrants."

By May 2009, Somerville's mayor and members of the elected School Committee had signed the pledge. People who had been among those approaching the mayor told me that he signed without hesitation. However, Somerville's Board of Aldermen refused to support the effort, and the overall initiative stalled.[6] City alderman Dick O'Neil told me in the summer of 2009 that local immigrant advocates had met with him individually to ask for his signature, but that the pledge "had such a political tone to it . . . was so divisive that it would really set off a political storm. I told them, 'The way it's written right now, I think you're going to have a rough time getting the support for this because it's more polarizing than it is welcoming.'" When I asked him to further explain his objection, O'Neil described the fallout from the 1987 Sanctuary City resolution: "People used that vote [to say] . . . 'You can come [to Somerville] and get away with anything you want? . . .' That was the perception that people are telling me people had."

At the same time as I heard objections to the Welcoming Somerville pledge, virtually everyone I talked with between 2007 and 2009—including elected officials, such as O'Neil, who had refused to take the pledge—spoke proudly of the city's history as a longtime gateway for immigrants. I suggest in Chapter 4 that this widespread identification with an immigrant heritage could be seen as an immigrant "imaginary" (Strauss 2006) that is used to emphasize a deprived immigrant past and masks current privilege and power. While a shared experience of immigration can serve to connect and ease tensions between older and newer immigrant generations in Somerville, it carries the danger of homogenizing and thus obscuring real and important inequalities in power and resources between these groups. Older generations may use the immigrant imaginary to justify a passive or even an openly oppositional stance toward policies and practices that would enable newer immigrants to become more fully incorporated into the political and public life of Somerville. As described in Chapter 1, such measures include routine language translation at city meetings, regular printing of city documents and public announcements made over the city's call system in multiple languages, routine voter registration drives in immigrant neighborhoods, multi-lingual ballots,[7] and extension to non-citizens the ability to vote in local elections.

Public statements by Somerville's popular, young mayor, a second-generation immigrant of Italian heritage, symbolize the city's commitment to an immigrant-friendly climate. A prime example is this declaration: "This is everybody's city who wants to live here, work hard, and make a positive contribution. I don't care what your status is" (Dreilinger 2007). This claim echoes this book's theme of social citizenship based on shared "values in which membership is open to all those who reside in a territory" (Glenn 2000: 3). The mayor also speaks with pride to and about the one-third of the city's residents who were born outside the United States and about the more than fifty languages spoken in the public schools (Carroll 2007).

On more than one occasion, I heard the mayor defend the city's newer immigrants and their neighborhood of East Somerville. At a ward meeting held on the city's west side, in largely white, affluent Davis Square, several residents called for a youth center in their neighborhood. He told them firmly: "A city youth center has to be centrally located so it's accessible to everyone in the city, not on the west side . . . and everything now has to take a back seat to rebuilding the East Somerville school [that recently burned in a fire]. . . . It serves a diverse community."

Later in that same meeting, a resident objected to a proposed new hotel that was being planned for Assembly Square in East Somerville because "I wouldn't put my guests there. There's lots of crime in that area." The mayor looked visibly annoyed and said, "Yeah, crime like at the Copley Hotel," referring to a recent high-profile murder that took place inside this luxury hotel, located in a very affluent neighborhood of Boston.

Somerville City Hall regularly holds official celebrations honoring the traditions of various immigrant groups (e.g., Haitian Flag Day, Central American Independence Day) and also displays artistic works and hosts musical performances by different immigrant groups. The city's museum frequently mounts exhibits documenting immigrant history and culture, such as the one described in Chapter 4, which my students and I became involved in during 2006 and 2007. City government has also on occasion provided various kinds of assistance to new immigrants seeking to remain in the United States legally. In 2006, City Hall was opened on a Saturday to allow the El Salvadoran Consulate to register eligible residents for temporary protected status that would allow them to stay in the United States for up to twelve months.

In addition to the mayor's expression of pro-immigrant sentiments and the city's sponsorship of various pro-immigrant activities, Somerville's new police chief, appointed in the summer of 2008, quickly established a reputation as being a friend to immigrants. Almost as soon as he arrived, the chief began to meet monthly with a group of immigrant advocates and service providers and the city's Human Rights Commission. His commitment to supporting new immigrants was particularly evident in April 2009, when he became a vocal public supporter of a newly proposed, controversial state-level policy to allow undocumented immigrants to obtain driver's licenses (Sacchetti 2009e).[8]

Latino and Haitian community leaders I interviewed who have lived in the city for over two decades generally saw the city as increasingly hospitable to immigrants. Chapter 4 presents quotations from newer immigrant leaders that make this point. Juliana Silva, a fifteen-year resident and community leader of Brazilian heritage, told me that immigrants feel safe in Somerville compared with other nearby towns:

> I think Somerville is still considered a sanctuary for immigrants. I think it's the mayor's commitment [and] the new [hired in 2008] police chief. He's great to work with. . . . [Somerville] police officers know the difficulty of getting a driver's license if you are undocumented, so they may give you a warning or a ticket but not necessarily call ICE on you because you don't have a driver's license. . . . [It's] different than the reputation of [a nearby town, which is] seen as dangerous for immigrants. So I think immigrants still feel safer in Somerville, and it's very scary times.

Tom Donahue, a local pastor (not himself an immigrant) whose congregation was largely made up of newer Latino immigrants, agreed, saying, "I think they feel comfortable here, especially if there's an [ICE] raid going on. I don't think they expect someone to say, 'Well, you don't have documents, so you can't rent a house here.'" Donahue also offered an example of how city officials protect local immigrants: "We had a meeting of the clergy with the mayor about two weeks ago, and one of the Brazilian pastors said he was asked for his green card by a city employee and the mayor said he wanted to know who that was [so he could follow up and correct the behavior]."

Alvarado Marquez, a Somerville resident for two decades, also saw the possibilities for more immigrant engagement in the city: "You don't need to be a citizen to make your voice heard. If you have a child in the school system, you can make noise with the School Committee."

Three Critical Local Events Calling Out Somerville Immigrant Engagement

Struggles over social citizenship (in terms of full membership in the community) give larger meaning to when and how immigrants become actively engaged in public affairs in Somerville. I identify two main factors conducive to their engagement. Those factors are the focus of the rest of this chapter: (1) critical local events that immediately threaten immigrants' safety and security and demand their attention and necessitate their involvement; and (2) an official local climate that immigrant leaders perceive as providing them with a relative measure of protection.

The first critical event that people I interviewed reported was a 1991 racial conflict at the local high school that occurred largely between the descendants of old-time (white) Irish immigrants and (black) Haitian newcomers. The second was the 2002 to 2004 passage of a Gang Ordinance that immigrant leaders see as especially threatening to Latino immigrant youth. The third critical event was the series of ongoing occasional raids by federal immigration agents that aimed primarily at undocumented Latino immigrants but affected anyone who "look[ed] Latino."

Event One: 1991 Racial Conflicts at Somerville High School

Ramon Vazquez described events that occurred during the early 1990s, when he was a student at Somerville High School. Ramon was born and raised in the city by his Latino first-generation immigrant parents: "In the nineties, when the race riots started after school and dragged out into the streets, you had some of these gangs, you know. You had this one gang that would wear Notre Dame hats, and it had ND as its symbol, which would stand for 'Nigger Dies.'"

A local newspaper described what happened at Somerville High School on February 1, 1991: "A race riot broke out in the [Somerville High School] cafeteria resulting in the suspension of more than a dozen students and the emergence of a new approach to race relations in the city" (Eisner 2001).

Reporting as Ramon had, the paper stated that students from longtime resident white families (identifying as Irish- and Italian-heritage Catholics) wore University of Notre Dame hats "because the ND . . . stood for 'Niggers Die,'" while (largely Haitian) black students wore University of Nevada-Las Vegas (UNLV) hats "which they said stood for 'Us Niggers Love Violence'" (Eisner 2001; respondent interviews by the author). According to the newspaper: "The teenagers were responding to changes in the city whose black population had more than tripled in a decade. In the 1980 census, Blacks . . . accounted for 2 percent of the city's residents. . . . By 1990, blacks accounted for 6 percent" (Eisner 2001). Most of those blacks were Haitian immigrants, as were the black students who took part in the incident at the high school.

The story differs as to what precipitated the "high school fight" as then-mayor (now U.S. Congressman) Michael Capuano preferred to call it, but people I talked with agreed that race was certainly an important aspect. As Dave Strong, who has lived in the city for twenty years and is a leader in the local schools, explained: "There was, for decades, a low-level hostility to newcomers [in Somerville], but when large numbers of immigrants started coming from Haiti and Central America, that triggered a lot of more overt hostility. . . . It became more aggressive. . . . Outright aggressive hostility focused on immigrants of color." Describing the high school incident for the local newspaper, the school headmaster recalled a history of "toughie ringleaders" taunting each other, while the then-mayor recalled that it "started out as typical high school stuff—boys fighting over girls—but at some point race became a factor" (Eisner 2001). Violence continued throughout the summer of 1991, although by autumn, the city had created the Somerville mediation program, credited with changing the climate in a positive direction. Ramon Vazquez reflected on the aftermath: "Once a lot of that stuff happened, but the city was changing already, but I think that opened the eyes of a lot of people. In some ways, I thought it brought harmony because they realized that their ways are getting people killed."

Somerville Haitian leader Vertus Bernique played a key role in providing a public space on the local community radio station for Haitian students to give voice to what they experienced:

[The students] called in. . . . [T]hey said they'd had enough. So many things had happened to them. The police would come and, without asking any questions, arrest them. They got beat up. They got humiliated by the teachers. And some of the boys were dating some of the white girls, and the brothers and sisters would get mad and beat them.

Following on this opportunity for Haitian youth's voices to be heard, Vertus described what he and others did next:

> We organized the community. A good number of people from the Haitian community, a hundred, I think, attended a meeting. . . . We had a plan and a strategy, and that's basically how the whole thing started about how to change things in Somerville. . . . The Human Rights Commission was started [in 1993] because of our organizing. Michael Capuano gave us advice, "You guys got to form an organization," and we've been doing that, building an organization. . . . We ask them to hire Haitian teachers. We ask that training be provided to the police. . . . [Now] there's less racial profiling and we have a black man as the police chief in Somerville . . . [and] the [current] mayor, he's a big voice for the immigrant community.

A number of people I talked with called up the events of 1991 as a key turning point for the city in terms of improving the climate for newer immigrant groups—an improvement that occurred at least in part because of the Haitian community's activism. Kevin Brennan, for example, a young leader of Irish heritage who was born and raised in the city, described to me his experience as a student in the city's high school right after 1991: "One of the things they did is to have a mediation program. When incidents happened, [school officials] brought the kids together and dealt with it directly. That program was a direct result of the riot."

Event Two: 2002 to 2004 Passage of a Gang Ordinance, Lingering Resentment among Latino Leaders and Advocates, and Pivotal Action by the New Police Chief

On October 24, 2002, two young deaf girls were raped in Somerville's Foss Park, near where most of the city's Latino residents live. Three members of what local people call an El Salvadoran gang were promptly arrested and threatened with deportation. The city responded by creating a police unit to address gang-related crime. When nervous residents subsequently accused the police chief of "non-existence of a phantom gang unit," he assigned three officers to what he called a "Gang Task Force dedicated solely to fighting gangs" (Chabot 2003).

Two months after the Foss Park rape, in December 2002, the Boston area's main newspaper reported that two Somerville city aldermen had begun drafting local anti-gang legislation. After a long and heated debate, the Gang Ordinance passed the Board of Aldermen on May 13, 2004. Three months later, on August 26, 2004, the lieutenant governor of Massachusetts signed it into law at a gathering in Foss Park (Gedan 2004).

Somerville's Gang Ordinance directs local police to order dispersal whenever they see "a member of a criminal street gang . . . loitering with one or more other persons," and to inform those persons "that they will be subject to arrest of they fail to obey." It mandates, "The Chief of Police shall . . . designate areas of the city [where] enforcement of this section is necessary." Gang loitering, being considered a member of a street gang, and being involved in criminal gang activity are defined in relation to someone the police consider to have

> intent to further the common purpose of a criminal street gang . . . [or someone who] engages in conduct which would cause a reasonable person to believe [that he or she may be subject to] inconvenience or hazard . . . defaces real or personal property . . . intimidates or accosts another, or engages in disorderly behavior or a breach of the peace. (Commonwealth of Massachusetts 2004)

Described by Boston's major metropolitan newspaper as "the first in the state . . . to give police broad authority to arrest suspected gang members who gather on city streets," the local ordinance was sharply criticized by Latino residents, who feared that "it would allow police to target all Latino teenagers" (Gedan 2004). Expressing an attitude about the neighborhood where many Latinos live, Somerville immigrant advocate Marleine Vera told me: "I've heard it that if you go into East Somerville, you don't want to be there, that there's so much violence, that it's an unsafe place in Somerville. There's this perception from the older Somerville residents that immigrants are bringing this lack of safety to the city and it's deteriorating the neighborhood."

Some East Somerville and other area residents supported the Gang Ordinance "because I'm definitely afraid to walk the streets" and claimed that "many of those who spoke against the ordinance did not have to deal with the threat of gang harassment or violence everyday" (Chabot 2002b). The local American Civil Liberties Union opposed the ordinance, stating that it "tramples on civil rights and may promote racial profiling" (Chabot 2002b).

Immigrant residents expressed concern that they themselves would be arrested at a bus stop or for simply speaking with a gang member on a street corner (Chabot 2002b). Local Latino activist Alvarado Marquez, who was involved in dialogues with local police at the time of the ordinance's passage, told me, "If I see a gang member and I decide to talk to them [*sic*] . . . the police can come and arrest me. That's against my civil rights." Alberto Dias, a prominent Latino leader who also talked with local police at the time, told me: "The city passed a law against gangs. . . . It was promoted by one of the aldermen, and the idea behind the law was that if three Latinos or two Latinos are talking on a corner, they could get arrested, and if three Italians are talking on a corner, they're fine."

Latinos were not the only ones who opposed the Gang Ordinance. Somerville youth leader and lifetime resident Kevin Brennan, who is white and Irish American, told me: "If they're committing a crime, arrest them, but this is the most densely packed city in New England, and it gets hot and people hang out in the parks after hours. What are you going to do, arrest them for hanging out? . . . So it's a false law and I don't like that it's on the table." Sandra Leavey, a two-decade resident who is an activist, a former city employee, and a middle-class professional, also opposed the Gang Ordinance, saying, "Young Latino men still have trouble hanging out on the corner in the way my young, white daughter has never been accosted by police for hanging out on the corner." Maria DeCosta is an Italian-heritage resident in her seventies who is actively engaged in the East Somerville neighborhood where she has lived her entire life. A fear of gangs might be understandable in her case because she is old enough to remember Somerville's twentieth-century legendary Winter Hill Gang. However, she took a different view:

> Well, there might actually be a gang problem, but no matter what happens in the city, whether it's a gang or not, they get blamed for it, and we all know who "they" means (i.e., immigrants, especially Latinos and/or those of color). . . . Personally, I have not seen gangs anywhere. They say they're on the corners. I look, I walk, I say I'm going out to see if there are gangs around. I don't see them. . . . So I think they embellish the idea of gangs.

On the other hand, Kevin Brennan told me:

> There is a gang situation going on in Somerville. There's always been gangs without the official gangs, and then there was the Winter Hill Gang, which was a real gang. Then there's MS-13, which is a real gang. They had people, adults, come to Somerville from El Salvador and organize in Somerville. . . . Then there's the Bloods and Crips thing . . . kids walking around in red or blue pretending to be Crips

and Bloods or whatnot. So they're pretending in the sense that there's no association with what's going on in L.A. and the real organizations. But it's very real violence. . . . So it's like fake gangs, real violence. When I grew up, if kids were fightin', they were doing it with fists. These kids, teenage kids, stab each other.

Three years after the proposal of the Gang Ordinance, the new (current) mayor reportedly still needed to take "steps to mend ties with immigrant communities" because he had "angered many Latinos" by promoting the controversial law (Gedan 2005). Some members of the city's progressive middle class, while they criticized the anti-immigrant thinking behind the ordinance, also saw it as an example of the mayor's effort to balance both his pro-immigrant sentiment and his loyalty to the city's "old guard." Steve Smith, a twenty-year Somerville resident and prominent immigrant advocate who regularly speaks with local officials, told me: "[The Gang Ordinance] is a good example of the concession [by city officials] to an old group of people who are afraid of immigrants. It is not clear the police are enforcing it, but it's still on the books. Some people would like the police to arrest, detain illegal immigrants, but they're not going to do that."

No one has ever been arrested for violating Somerville's Gang Ordinance. However, in March 2009, an incident occurred between six Latino male Somerville High School students and local police that suggested that the ordinance still has salience for both police and immigrants. On March 10, 2009, six Latino male Somerville High School students who were on their way home from school walked past youths who were having a fight. As the six students, fifteen to eighteen years of age, tried to cross the street to avoid the fight, police stopped them and accused them of being members of a gang called the Latin Kings. Police ordered all six young men to spread-eagle, place their palms against the side of a police cruiser, and drop to their knees. Two of the youth claimed that police had bashed their heads against a police cruiser, an accusation the police denied (Smith 2009a).

Somerville Human Rights Commissioners questioned the police chief about this incident a few days later, at its regular monthly March meeting. The chief immediately opened an investigation. At a Human Rights Commission meeting I attended a month later, a Latino commissioner reported that the alleged police actions against the six Latino youth were "against everything [the chief] stands for." This commissioner was an active participant in a group established by local immigrant leaders and their allies, called the Immigrant Dialogue Group, which met with the police chief every month.

Meanwhile, before the police investigation could be completed, the Board of Aldermen passed a resolution (without mentioning the incident) that expressed general support for the Somerville police and stated that they should have all the tools they need to fight gangs. At that meeting, one of Somerville's longtime "old guard" alderman, who supported the resolution, and a young, progressive alderman elected only a few years before, who opposed it, engaged in a shouting match as an uproar ensued (Nash 2009a). At the same time, several prominent city leaders spoke out publicly to support the character of one or more of the six young Latino students. Among these supporters were the mayor, who knew some of the youth from his years of coaching football at the high school, and the Latino youth coordinator at the city's community action agency (Smith 2009a).

By the end of April, the police chief had completed his investigation. From now on, he decreed, police policy would be that officers must be "one hundred percent sure" before accusing youth of being gang members (Smith 2009b). Police would receive new training to distinguish between youth fights and gang activity, an issue that had loomed large when the Gang Ordinance was passed five years earlier. Although the chief found no evidence that any of his officers had used undue force, he disciplined a police officer who used profanity at the scene. None of the youths were arrested.

While the chief had managed not to undermine the authority of his officers, he had also chosen not to use the Gang Ordinance in ways that the parents of the Latino boys feared. At the same time, the whole event had served to enflame racial-ethnic and generational conflicts that both still divide the city of Somerville.

Event Three: 2007 and 2008 Immigration and Customs Enforcement Raids

Like other cities throughout the United States with sizable new immigrant (especially Latino) populations, Somerville was targeted during the period of my research by federal Immigration and Customs Enforcement (ICE) raids in 2007 and 2008. As white, middle-class activist Sandra Leavey, a former city employee, put it, "ICE raids terrorized Somerville." In just four months, from June to September 2008, federal ICE agents arrested 114 Massachusetts immigrants, most of whom were in the United States legally. (Recall the fifty-one conditions under which legal as well as undocumented immigrants can be deported.) According to federal officials, all except one of these 114 had a record of being arrested (but not necessarily convicted) of various crimes (Sacchetti 2008a). During 2007, federal immigration officials deported 3,836 immigrants from New England, an increase from 3,464 the year before (Sacchetti 2008a).

These facts provide clear reasons for the fear experienced by anyone perceived by ICE as looking like an immigrant. That most often means anyone with brown skin, whether a U.S. citizen, a legal non-citizen, or an unauthorized resident.[9] When people in Somerville hear that ICE agents have entered the city, panic ensues in heavily Latino neighborhoods (Aizenman 2007; Cooper 2007). This panic, and the active efforts by immigrant leaders and their allies and advocates to deal with it, increased in Somerville after a highly publicized raid on a factory in New Bedford, Massachusetts, where ICE detained 361 workers charged with being in the United States illegally (Ballon 2008; Dreilinger 2008a, 2008b; Mohr 2008).[10] On August 28, 2007, federal immigration agents raided a Somerville auto body shop, arresting an employee they claimed was an MS-13 gang member. The owner of the shop said the agents told him that it was not an immigration raid and that they were after only this one individual. Still, they lined up all the other employees and checked their immigration status (Hassett 2007b). In response to these kinds of incidents, local immigrant leaders and advocates proposed a "rapid response network . . . to get information out quickly in the aftermath of ICE operations in the city" (Hassett 2007d). While some voiced concerns about the dangers of teaching immigrants "how to evade or avoid the law," people at a community meeting cheered when leaders proposed the network (Hassett 2007d).

ICE agents entered the city again in August 2008. Reports circulated that they were stopping people at a local subway station as they got off trains at the end of the work day as well as at a Dunkin' Donuts that was well known as a community gathering place in the city's east side, which was heavily populated by Latino residents. Local immigrant leaders and advocates moved quickly to meet with Somerville's police chief, who said that he had already asked his officers to file a report with him if they assisted any ICE agent. The chief had also asked ICE agents to give him the names of any Somerville residents who were arrested, and he had agreed to immediately notify the city's Human Rights Commission with information about arrests (Dreilinger 2008a).

Immigrant leaders and advocates further urged the chief to change his own policy of notifying ICE if an undocumented resident was arrested for a serious crime within the city limits. An immigrant leader active in the Immigrant Dialogue Group[11] reported to me in October that "The police in Somerville have committed to not report to ICE unless they need to. We meet with [the police] and get commitments." While immigrant activists were gratified by these measures, some wanted city officials to openly condemn the presence of ICE agents and their actions, even though they understood that city officials did not have the authority to stop them.

At meetings of the Human Rights Commission that I attended in late summer and fall of 2008, members reported that they were "keeping our eye" on reports that a city resident had been arrested in the raids and was being deported. Commission members also reported about the bi-monthly meetings and activities of the Immigrant Support Network, which "serve[s] as a support center for immigrants affected by raids by providing legal, political, and financial aid" (Nicas 2008a). The Network emerged as a rapid response network after the 2007 ICE raids. It is a collaboration of local immigrant rights organization Centro Presente and a new group called Voices for Immigrants in Somerville that was organized by the city's community development organization. As immigrant activist Marleine Vera, who was involved in forming the Immigrant Support Network, explained to me, "The network came after there was a series of two raids [and] six or seven people from Somerville were detained. That really riled people up, and they wanted to do something about it. . . . Unfortunately, we know that more [raids] are going to happen. It happens regularly in Somerville." Local Latino churches were among the important venues for the network's information sessions, which were often offered at the churches after Sunday morning services.

Also in response to the August 2008 raids, Centro Presente immediately organized vigils and several press conferences, including one on Boston City Hall Plaza (Nash 2008). I attended a press conference held at a Somerville Latino church, where a staff member from Centro Presente declared, "We are here to denounce the presence of ICE in our community. We need an immigration policy to reflect liberty . . . [to reflect] that it is not a crime to be an immigrant trying to support your family." The church's minister, a highly visible local immigrant leader and owner of several successful immigrant businesses in Somerville, spoke next: "I'm an immigrant, just like the people being chased. I'm a victim of the war in El Salvador. . . . I came here because they were trying to kill me, [and] I came here to work. . . . We do the jobs that nobody else wants to touch." The minister was followed by an older, soft-spoken Latino man, also Salvadoran, accompanied by a small child in a stroller. He was dressed in work clothes and spoke in Spanish, saying, "I want to ask ICE to stop the raids. They come early in the morning and take the mothers and the fathers."

The threat of ICE raids and resulting arrest and deportation, while offering the occasion and impetus for civic engagement on behalf of immigrants, also has a chilling effect, not only in Somerville but also in other U.S. cit-

ies and towns (Ramakrishnan and Bloemraad 2008b: 67). A 2007 Pew Hispanic Center study found that more than one-half of Latinos worry that
they, a family member, or a friend may be deported (Cordero-Guzman,
Martin, and Quiroz-Becerra 2008: 603). Over and over, people told me that
immigrants in Somerville, especially but not only undocumented ones, were
too afraid to come out and be visibly active in community issues or even to
report abuses on the job that threatened their health and safety (Dreilinger
2008a). Dave Strong, a twenty-year resident and local leader who now holds
an elected city post, made this comment, which was frequently heard: "The
anti-immigrant sentiment and the ICE raids have really driven people under-
ground. The immigrant community is less well organized politically and
institutionally less powerful publicly. It's a shame. There were more immigrant organizations ten years ago than there are now." Echoing this view,
Juliana Silva told me:

> This year, I'm very worried about the children in the school. A couple
> of the small kids, one parent has been taken [by federal agents]. . . .
> We work with the families, and it's so devastating. The middle
> school kids, just think how many people do they know who've been
> arrested, how many family members who've been arrested.

This fear threatens what progress has been made in the city in terms of
immigrant groups and their level of civic engagement.

Extending Social Citizenship: Changes That
Could Support Greater Inclusion and Engagement
of Immigrants in Local Public Affairs

Immigrant participation in public affairs at the local level, when it occurs,
creates a firm foundation for incorporating immigrants as full members of
the community—that is, for social citizenship and participation in shared
governance as a form of democracy. Having large numbers of immigrant residents who are "non-participating, unrepresented, [and] disengaged" poses a
threat to democracy more generally (Andersen 2008: 77).

A number of immigrant activists and their advocates and allies I talked
with in the summer and fall of 2008, such as Dave Strong, who was quoted
earlier, saw a decline in immigrant engagement in Somerville compared with
earlier years. They all traced this decline to immigrants' fear of arrest or
deportation or both. Juliana Silva confirmed Dave's impression that Somerville immigrants were sometimes too afraid to become actively involved in

community affairs: "It's very scary, so people are not stepping forward. . . . It's not the time, especially if you're undocumented. They're even arresting people with green cards." At the same time, without Somerville's relatively welcoming and protective climate, compared with cities with a more hostile climate, immigrant engagement would likely not occur, even at the level it does. Tom Donahue, pastor of a local church attended largely by Salvadorans, called attention to both of these factors when I asked what would get members of his congregation out to a community meeting: "Issues of immigration [would get them out] as long as they felt comfortable being there. That's why sometimes Centro Presente will call and say, 'Can we have a meeting here [at the church]?' Because they feel comfortable here."

What I learned from actively engaged Somerville immigrants and their allies is, then, that critical local events that threaten the safety and security of immigrants and the fear they cause both dampen and call forth active engagement. A strong example of this is how raids by ICE and their accompanying threat of arrest and deportation (even for legal immigrants) have had a chilling effect over time on immigrant participation in public life in Somerville. At the same time, these raids have been important occasions for increased engagement and organizing by immigrant leaders and their allies and advocates. A recent national study of immigrant protest reports a similar finding: that threats against immigrants tend to encourage protest (Okamoto and Ebert 2010).

Overall, then, this chapter shows that active and organized participation in community affairs by immigrants, however limited, does take place. Immigrants do become civically and politically active, to some extent, around issues that affect them. At the same time, the relatively lesser immigrant engagement around commonly shared citywide issues, such as the major ongoing redevelopment projects, suggests that immigrants are not full members of their community. If they had full access to membership and acceptance, to social citizenship, they could instead "act autonomously . . . for the common good, rather than out of . . . immediate material needs" (Glenn 2000: 7).

Even though some amount of immigrant engagement occurs in Somerville, the city's newer immigrant groups (some of whom have lived in the city for over two decades) have not even begun to gain a foothold in elected positions in city government. These positions are not completely closed. As of 2009, a number of middle-class professionals have begun to make inroads into local politics. One of the city's eleven aldermen is from this "newcomer" group, as are four of the nine School Committee members.

People told me that becoming legal citizens and being able to vote are key components of what is needed to empower new immigrants. Research shows that voting is connected to other forms of civic engagement (Flanagan, Levine, and Settersten 2008). Some of the immigrant leaders I spoke with, such as Alberto Dias, suggested that residents should be able to vote in local elections, even if they are not U.S. citizens: "If you're a resident, you're on your way to citizenship. You're obligated to pay taxes, everything a citizen pays. Non-citizens have children that are born here; they own homes here. . . . I think they should be entitled to decide who is going to govern them." Sheila Gayner, civic leader in her neighborhood of East Somerville, where most of the city's newer immigrants live, also said that voting is key to incorporating newcomers into the public life of the city and to policies that would facilitate immigrant voting: "I think the big challenge for the immigrant groups is that they have to have enough people who are voters. . . . In East Somerville, the largest voting bloc is made up of senior citizens, and so, until [new immigrants] start registering to vote, I don't see change." Pastor of an immigrant church, Tom Donahue told me, "I tell people where to go and register, get out there and vote." Sean Russo, a longtime elected city official, spoke of how being a voter is essential to gaining influence in the city: "When I go door-to-door, and you have to go door-to-door in this city to get elected, I take with me a list of registered voters. I look at a house, see no registered voters, and go right by it. So if you want to have influence in this city, register, vote, and participate."

Immigrant leaders and their allies and advocates have put forth a number of ideas, in addition to allowing non-citizens to vote in local elections, for changes in local policy and practice that would facilitate increased voting by immigrants. Steve Smith said, "They can put the ballots in different languages and . . . do voter education. Put civics back into the schools, have mail ballots, provide computers in the libraries where people can use them to vote, have someone to organize an effort to try to get some of these [newer immigrant] folks to run for office." As I have said before, some U.S. cities have instituted some of these suggestions as ways to facilitate immigrant engagement locally, especially practices that remove barriers to non–English speakers, such as requiring city offices to include bilingual staff, having public notices that announce public meetings and communicate other public matters in multiple languages, having local ballot questions printed in multiple languages, and so forth (De Graauw 2008).

Largely missing in Somerville during the period of my research were immigrant leaders and organizations engaged in developing a well-articulated strategy to mobilize newer immigrants to become involved in local politics. Other research has found that mobilization is critically important to the political incorporation of immigrants (Bloemraad 2006).[12] Latinos in other cities in Massachusetts have had some success in gaining elected political positions, and their experience also suggests measures that could be adopted or greatly expanded in Somerville (Hardy-Fanta and Gerson 2002). These include organizing youth and parents around the schools, where new immigrant groups are typically overrepresented among students and parents; establishing local immigrant-based newspapers and radio and television stations; emphasizing a district-based system of local government; encouraging Latino candidates to run in areas with large numbers of Latino voters; drawing on immigrant leaders who staff immigrant service organizations to run for office; and registering eligible immigrant groups and encouraging them to vote. These strategies can be integrated into immigrant service provision, advocacy, and neighborhood and housing organizing efforts.

Some of these strategies are emerging in Somerville. Those I talked with recognize that organizing immigrants through the public schools can form a basis for political mobilization. The Welcome Project has begun working with immigrant parents, and those parents have begun talking with school officials about initiatives to better support their children's aspirations for college. A few immigrant leaders, such as the Haitian leader during the 1991 high school conflict, are making good use of the local community television station. Some community organizations in Somerville have successfully recruited more immigrant staff and board members, and some of them could be actively groomed to run for local political office.

Some local organizations are also conducting programs with the potential to increase immigrant engagement in the city and eventually to support people from newer immigrant groups to run for and achieve public office. Somerville's community development agency runs several programs aimed at building leadership among newer immigrants. The Welcome Project and Centro Presente offer English language classes, with civic engagement as a topic. Centro Presente also teaches new immigrant residents about city politics, hosts local candidate nights, and runs voter registration campaigns. The Welcome Project and Centro Presente both run immigrant youth empowerment programs that reach out to immigrant parents to involve them in community affairs. Although they are not aimed directly at bringing newer immigrant groups into public office, these initiatives have the potential to create a political base.

A major challenge to a coordinated immigrant mobilization strategy in Somerville, compared with surrounding towns, such as Lowell (which recently elected its first Latino mayor), is the multiplicity of different racial-ethnic and language groups in Somerville. The largest immigrant groups are Latinos, Brazilians, and Haitians, who all speak different languages. As Haitian resident Monique Clovet told me, "I think all the immigrants should really work together, which we don't have."[13] And as Alvarado Marquez said, "There's a lot of disconnection between Latinos living in Somerville."

Should Somerville immigrants become less engaged on their own behalf, with the support of immigrant advocates and allies, the city's relatively welcoming climate would likely decline. As young immigrant activist Marleine Vera told me:

> There's a lot of interest [in immigrant issues] on the part of elected officials and the higher-up people in the city . . . but . . . making sure that those issues are addressed is on the [immigrant] community. So if the community is not organizing and constantly pushing . . . bringing these things up, then even those concerned, it goes to the back burner. . . . [T]he mayor, even though he's concerned, [won't] actually do something unless there are people at his door.

As important as the active engagement by immigrant leaders is, for Somerville's current political power structure to change to include formal immigrant representation, immigrant leaders (and non-immigrants who support them) must develop an explicit political mobilization strategy. In the absence of such a strategy, immigrant concerns in Somerville, as elsewhere in the United States, are far less likely to be heard and addressed (American Political Science Association 2004: 11; Hardy-Fanta and Martinez 2002). I discuss this further in Chapter 7.

6

Gentrification, Resident Displacement, and a Common Vision for the City's Future

Against a background of debates about immigrant incorporation, economic development, gentrification, and resident displacement, this chapter gives evidence of a shared vision for Somerville's future reaching across the city's three main social divides.[1] This commonality was also evident in the community visions for the city, discussed in Chapter 3, where the main priorities in both a vision emerging from a process led by a grassroots community-based coalition and one led by the city administration were resident diversity, affordable housing, and economic development aimed at enhancing the city's tax base.

Somerville is at a critical turning point, where city government and its actively engaged residents are making numerous decisions about the future. As they make these decisions, one of their major challenges is maximizing the positive effects of gentrification while being aware of the negative effects. On the one hand, this centuries-old city needs new commercial and residential development and new transportation projects to attract new businesses and middle-class residents. City Hall staff reported to me in the fall of 2010 that three-fourths of the city's 2009 budget came from residential property taxes, a figure substantially higher than that for other cities in the region.[2] Somerville's city administration claims that new, more affluent residents will bring much needed revenue to the city and improve the quality of life for all. At the same time, the administration and actively engaged residents alike acknowledge that many working-class and low-income residents of Somerville have already been displaced by gentrification. As activist Dave Strong told me, "Our poor and working-class people are being driven out. More will likely suffer the same fate as the city continues its plans for community development." Mike Kent, who heads a key community organization in the city, said: "The big question is can we try to do some things . . . like new transit amenities, new development in economically undeveloped parts of the city . . . but not lose the economical and racial diversity that we have in the process." At a June 2008 meeting of agency heads and city officials, the then–executive director of the Somerville's community action agency expressed this same dilemma: "On the one hand, we've got gentrification, and then also an immigrant population who are low income. . . . How to keep both diversity and gentrification is the main challenge." This concern was expressed repeatedly in my interviews, at community meetings, and in local newspapers at the time (Federico 2009a).

Urban scholars coined the term "gentrification" in the mid-1960s (Hannigan 1995: 174). It describes a process that began when housing in old industrial cities like Somerville declined and deteriorated, along with the loss of the industrial economy. New owners and real estate developers began to upgrade housing and made large financial gains by selling to more affluent new residents. Perhaps the most well studied urban process since the 1970s (Hackworth 2002: 815), gentrification is defined in multiple and competing ways:

> To some gentrification epitomizes needed revitalization . . . to others gentrification represents destruction of longstanding communities. . . . The difference between "revitalization" and "gentrification" has been delineated as "when property values and rents rise to the point that longstanding residents are pushed out . . . because they can no longer afford the rents or property taxes" (Knotts and Haspel 2006: 110, 114).

Scholars who focus on the revitalization and rehabilitation aspects of gentrification emphasize how new neighborhoods attract an affluent middle class, which then becomes a source of much-needed revenue to support city services, an idea I heard expressed often by Somerville officials (Betancur 2002; Lees 2008). Proponents of gentrification prefer the less controversial term "urban renaissance" (Lees 2008: 2452). They celebrate middle-class residents who move into revitalized urban areas as a new urban creative class or as new urban pioneers who choose to live in cosmopolitan urban centers instead of homogeneous suburbs (Florida 2005; Hannigan 1995; Lees 2008).

Others are more concerned with the negative aspects of gentrification, especially the displacement (or replacement) of working-class residents that occurs as middle- and upper-income residents move into lower-income urban neighborhoods. Displacement occurs when people are forced to leave their homes because of rising rents or property taxes, or when lower-income and working-class people cannot move into a neighborhood because of these costs (Griffith 1995: 249). Residents who are at risk for being displaced sometimes actively resist (Hackworth 2002), and some research shows that lower-income suburbs (which some would consider Somerville to be) are "much more likely than other types of places to mobilize in favor of growth control" (Nguyen 2009: 39). The displacement literature also focuses on class and race conflict among working-class residents (white or of color) and the middle-class gentrifiers (usually white) (Betancur 2002; Perez 2002).

I discuss the Somerville redevelopment projects that threaten gentrification-caused displacement in Chapter 3. Recall the huge 145-acre, flat, open riverfront plot of land called Assembly Square, located in the eastern part of Somerville, an area populated mostly by lower-income newer immigrants. Plans for that area include a large IKEA store, a city park, a block of 2,100 new residential units, retail and office space, shops, restaurants, and a two-hundred-room hotel (OSPCD 2008: iv). This ambitious project, slated for completion by 2019, will form a completely new neighborhood.

The city's historic Union Square is being redeveloped as the city's main center. Consistent with new thinking about city cores as centers of entertainment and culture and residential districts instead of traditional "business" districts (Strom 2008), Union Square will contain a new arts center and housing designated for low-income artists. As city arts leader Mark Lewis (who might be characterized as part of a new urban creative class) told me, "The mayor thinks that artists can come into Union Square and make it attractive and help redevelopment. . . . He's expecting some sort of payoff, with the arts community making Union Square more of a destination." The role of the arts is seen as a key driver of gentrification in old working-class neighborhoods, such as Union Square (Cameron and Coaffee 2005). Somerville claims that 4.5 percent of its residents (four times the national average) are artists of one kind or another, including writers, editors, architects, graphic designers, and musicians (Fairclough 2008).

Important new transportation initiatives are part of both of these projects. Assembly Square, bordering directly on Boston city limits, will have a new subway station. Union Square will have an entirely new subway stop.

These improvements are expected to increase the number of people moving to Somerville because these stations will connect directly and quickly to Boston proper, offering easy access to jobs and cultural and educational resources.[3] The Union Square Green Line extension, discussed in Chapter 3, will provide easy access to neighborhoods east and west across Somerville. These transportation improvements are also expected to keep young, middle-class people in the city, perhaps converting them from renters to homeowners. When I talked with him in June 2009, ten-year resident, current renter, and young professional Mark Lewis was looking, with his wife, for a house to buy in Union Square: "They say the [subway Green Line] is coming, and we like the idea of being more connected to public transportation. It's supposed to run through Union Square and then up to Tufts [University], and so we're looking at the neighborhoods where [there are] proposed stops and considering those as options." In Somerville today, much political and civic engagement occurs around these key sites of large-scale economic redevelopment, as earlier explored. Active residents want to retain locally owned smaller businesses and keep the relatively modest character and appearance of the city (e.g., having new buildings with relatively small footprints and low heights).

In this chapter, I focus on active engagement around gentrification and the feared loss of affordable housing that will push out working-class and lower-income residents. Later, I contend that while the city's tensions between old and new residents, between the working class and the middle class, and between white ethnics and newer immigrants of color play out around these development-related issues, they are not at the root of the city's most fundamental conflict, which is the struggle for local political power. This topic is the focus of Chapter 7.

Gentrification, Rising Housing Costs, and Resident Displacement

When I interviewed both older working-class white ethnics and newer immigrants of color, they told me that they or their parents or grandparents settled in Somerville in large part because housing was (and to some extent still is) affordable. Andrade Coelho, whose parents brought him to Somerville from Portugal over fifty years ago, when he was a small child, said, "Folks would come, and this was a place they could live for a while. They could rent fairly cheaply, and then they could buy." Ramon Vazquez, a lifelong resident in his mid-thirties who was born in Somerville of immigrant parents, said that his parents chose this city in the early 1980s because "they could buy a house in Somerville. It was affordable." Middle-class professionals like Sam Martin also moved to Somerville for reasons that were economic: "I had lived in Cambridge and my family started to expand and I couldn't afford it, so I moved" in 1978.

Into the 1980s, Somerville was still a place where low-income, working-class, and less affluent middle-class residents could find relatively low-cost housing. This has gradually changed as average rent for a two-bedroom apartment more than doubled, from $301 to $821, from 1982 to 1996 (Shelton 2005). A statewide resolution that was passed in 1996 ending rent control contributed to dramatic increases in housing costs. For the most part, residents of the urban eastern region of Massachusetts that includes Boston and Somerville did not vote to end rent control, but voters in the state's more suburban and rural western region did.

The loss of rent control opened Somerville to rent increases. Still, Somerville had more available rental housing than neighboring Cambridge, so rents did not rise as rapidly in Somerville. The huge rapid rise in the cost of existing housing did not happen as early or as widely in Somerville. Because of these factors, Somerville remained more affordable than other places, even as Somerville's housing costs rose.

Large numbers of displaced residents from Cambridge and some areas of Boston moved to Somerville in the late 1990s, causing a "housing boom" (Powers and Danseyar 2001). This resulted in a housing shortage that further drove up rising Somerville housing costs (Powers and Danseyar 2001). In the five short years between 2000 and 2005, the median value of owner-occupied housing units in Somerville doubled, from $214,100 to $435,200, just as it had done earlier in Cambridge and areas of Boston. During this time, the cost of housing in Somerville was rising nine times faster than median income (Shelton 2005).

Between 1999 and 2003, two of Somerville's zip codes were among the top twenty local areas with rapidly increasing home prices (Swidley 2004). The year 2004 saw Somerville's first-ever sale of a million-dollar single-family home, one of the city's beautiful old Victorians built by the city's original affluent Yankee founders at the turn of the twentieth century (Parker 2004). In one year, from 2004 to 2005, 578 new Somerville condo units were created, a 70 percent increase over the previous year (Hassett 2008a). Condo conversion further contributed to the scarcity of rental housing in a city where two-thirds of Somerville housing units are occupied by renters, not homeowners (U.S. Census Bureau 2000b). While new condos decrease the number of available rentals, they also increase tax revenues because their value is typically higher than that of rental properties (Hassett 2008d). The cost of housing continued to rise until 2008, when, as in other regions and cities around the United States, the value of housing began to decline.

At the same time as costs rose, Somerville housing designated as "affordable" in the 1980s was undergoing what is called "expiring use," meaning that, after a certain number of years, housing originally designated as affordable reverts to market value.[4] Because the city's housing department and owners and/or developers made these agreements in the 1980s to expire in twenty years, expiring use took effect just as other factors in 2000 caused huge increases in housing costs (e.g., Powers and Danseyar 2001).

Another watershed event that contributed to rising real estate costs in Somerville in the late 1980s was the 1984 opening of Somerville's first (and still only) stop on the region's rail subway transportation system. The new subway stop opened in what is now Somerville's most affluent area, called Davis Square (Ackerman 2007). Since the mid-1980s, Davis Square has gradually become a lively spot, with quality restaurants, a theater for first-run films and live performances, trendy boutiques, and coffee shops—all signaling that Somerville was on the path to becoming an attractive place to live. Urban scholars have documented the importance of new upscale restaurants, cafés, and stores as visible signs of gentrification in cities all over the world (Zukin 2009).[5] In 2005, the Boston region's major newspaper reported that this had happened in Somerville:

> For several decades, this four-square-mile city with 80,000 residents has been plagued with low household incomes, poor transportation, and sparse and uneven commercial development. Since the 1980's, Davis Square near Tufts University has blossomed, fed by a new Red Line T stop, and a hot housing market (Diesenhouse 2005).

The article also reported a remark made by the new mayor, then in his second year of office: "Outsiders used to look down on us as 'Slumerville,' a city of scrap yards and corruption. Now we're reviving Somerville pride." In 2008, Boston's major newspaper described this still relatively new picture of Somerville: "Home to many artists and forward-thinking types, the city teems with energy, hosting farmer's markets and festivals. The population is very diverse . . . and the city's young energetic mayor is helping to shed the city's rough image" (Green 2008). A 2009 article described Somerville as one of the region's "top spots to live . . . for hipsters," describing it as a city that "embraces its bohemian side [with] quirky festivals . . . factories and other buildings converted into studios for artists . . . loads of restaurants and bars, as well as venues for indie music acts . . . [all] making the city cool enough to banish the epithet 'Slumerville' forever" (Gehrman 2009; see also Knight 2006).

People I interviewed who had lived in the city long enough to observe these changes saw them as related to resident displacement. Andrea Ferro, born in Somerville and still living in the Portuguese neighborhood where her parents first settled when they came from the Azores in the early 1950s, said, "The way the city has gone, with all these condos and the costs of homes, we've pushed a lot of people out." Vertus Bernique, a Haitian leader and twenty-year resident, told me: "We are losing Latin people and Haitians. They are moving. The housing is too expensive for them. The Haitian community is settling in Everett, and some move all the way to Brockton. They go where they can afford." Thirty-year resident Alberto Dias, who came to Somerville alone as a young man to escape the violence in Central America, observed that Latinos "have moved to Lynn, Everett, Malden, Medford, East Boston—to buy houses because they are less expensive. Taxes are not as high as they are in Somerville." Alvarado Marquez, who has lived in the city for over two decades and recently bought a two-family house in East Somerville, told me: "I think many people have moved in the past fifteen years because of the real estate, the rent, and the price of houses. A lot of us are struggling to stay in Somerville. . . . Development is good for some people, but . . . it's not good for other people." Objective evidence supports these perceptions. A 2009 city survey showed that the main reason why people moved from Somerville was because they could not afford to buy or rent homes (OSPCD 2009b: 20).

Andrade Coelho, quoted earlier, said, "What's happened now is that the real estate is boxing out a lot of people who can't afford to live here, recent immigrants." Andrade was not optimistic about Somerville's capacity to hold on to its racial-ethnic and class diversity in the face of gentrification, saying, "I think the pressures to gentrify are immense . . . unless the city develops a plan, a serious plan. . . . But I think economics are eventually just gonna win." Although Isabel Garcia, a forty-year-old Latina resident of Somerville since 1992 who had been living for the past ten years in the city's public housing for low-income people, saw her city changing and growing, she said:

> I don't see it growing for the people who are low-income. I see it prospering for people that are middle-class with more money. . . . If you see this plan for all these condominiums, I am like, "Wow, this is for people that have a lot of money," but what about the people that don't? What about people like me that have a dream to buy a home and have a backyard?

Less affluent, older, white ethnic residents from the city's longtime working class also worry about their own displacement. Rosemary O'Hanrahan, a lifelong resident who is a second-generation immigrant of Irish heritage and is in her seventies, had this to say: "I couldn't live here myself if it weren't for the fact that I live [in subsidized elderly housing]. The only [older] people who can make it are the ones who bought a house [a long time ago, when prices were low]." Maria DeCosta, a lifelong, second-generation resident of Italian heritage who is also in her seventies, shared a similar view: "For people of low income, we don't have enough housing [and] I don't see that getting better in the plans they are making in Union Square." In a powerful statement about what is lost when a working-class neighborhood gentrifies, Kevin Brennan, a thirty-year-old, third-generation resident of Irish heritage who is a youth leader and was born and raised in the city, told me: "The gentrification process, we never saw it until it was right in our faces. Suddenly, everything changed. We didn't know people on the street anymore. We were strangers in our own community."

These comments suggest that displacement results in more than the loss of a home. It also can be a shattering experience, caused by and leading to a loss of community. When I asked Kevin why the people who used to live on his street left, he said:

> It's the housing market. . . . They were forced out or they sold their houses to get ahead. . . . A lot of people moved out for the money, but they still have this identity toward Somerville. We have a friend who's been living in Everett for the last fifteen years and he's in Somerville every day, and if you ask him where he's from, he's from Somerville.

Middle-class professional Sam Martin, who has lived and worked in Somerville for over thirty years, told me that these concerns extend across class, race-ethnicity, and generations of old and new immigrants, although not without some measure of tension:

> The white working-class part of the city tended initially to see the [newer] immigrants as competition. Now they see that everybody is in the same boat. . . . There's this group [of people] called Save Our Somerville . . . [who see that they] have the same problems of being pushed out of the city by increasing prices. [They see] that affordable housing benefits both working-class whites and the immigrants.

Young founders of a voluntary association called Save Our Somerville (SOS) are lifelong, working-class residents of Irish heritage whose goal is "to begin a discussion about gentrification in Somerville and the negative impacts of rising property values which are driving out the blue-collar and immigrant character of the city." One told me about how his family had been forced out of their home by a rent increase, and about being treated as an outsider by some of the new, more affluent residents: "It's just weird when you walk around the neighborhood and they don't look at you. . . . You can tell when it is someone from around here because they will look you in the eyes."

The SOS founders believe that some of the actively engaged middle-class newcomers to the city share a vision of the city remaining affordable, and so SOS wants to collaborate both with newer immigrant groups and with those middle-class gentrifiers "who want to talk about preserving some of the character of the city and keeping it affordable . . . even as changes occur" (Parker 2005c). Sam Martin also talks about middle-class gentrifiers who share common concerns with both longtime, white, ethnic residents and newer immigrant groups of color: "The gentrifiers are also speaking out about this and doing something."

One such gentrifier is young, middle-class professional Mark Lewis, who (like Andrea, Vertus, Alberto, Andrade, Isabel, Rosemary, Maria, and Kevin) worries about people (including himself) being forced out: "I think Somerville is going to become a more and more desirable place to live, and it's going to become more expensive. I hope it doesn't become like some of the more expensive neighborhoods in Boston or Cambridge. . . . It's going to take some very clever people to figure out how to make sure that doesn't happen."

It is clear, then, both from engaged residents' accounts and from statistical evidence that, since the 1980s, Somerville has experienced rapidly rising housing costs and subsequent resident displacement. Along with some degree of consensus about a vision for the city's future, not surprisingly, displacement has at times caused overt conflict. Professional, middle-class, twenty-year resident Peter Evans said that some older working-class, white, ethnic residents "feel really possessive and feel like it's their territory." Sam Martin spoke about times when "the older people . . . with working-class jobs . . . who grew up here . . . had angry confrontations with [middle-class newcomers], with their expensive strollers and their toddlers."

Sam recalls an incident a local newspaper reported in October 2005 about a youth arrested in the city for spraying on a city wall the phrase "Kill a Yuppie," which stands for young urban professional (Gregory 2005; Shelton 2005). The youth lived in a city just north of Somerville that was known as a place where working-class and low-income Somerville residents move when they can no longer afford to live in Somerville. Another example of graffiti read, "Yuppies are to us as the Pilgrims were to the Indians."

The online postings that followed this arrest are characteristic of class con-flicts that often surround gentrification. One poster wrote, "Gentrification is going on in most cities surrounding Boston. . . . It's called progress." This was followed by, "Progress for who? So new people can move in. This prog-ress you talk about is cause for more families struggling to get by. How does this progress help the families that this city was built on?" And another: "If there's a rent hike, then move." A local blog exchange in August 2008 ex-hibited conflict between longtime working-class residents and middle-class newcomers. One said, "People moving here [are] pushing the price of hous-ing beyond what longtime residents can pay." An unsympathetic responder wrote, "This is America, and people are free to move in and out of neigh-borhoods as they please. If you can't afford to live in Somerville, then move somewhere you can afford" (Comments 2008).

Rosario Gonzales, a first-generation, middle-class, Latina immigrant, told me about white middle-class gentrifiers who did not want to associate with her or other people of color: "These newcomers . . . they feel like they own the whole world, and they . . . have the perception that they just want to be surrounded by white rich people. They want to be around the color white instead of any other color."

Suggesting that at least some white middle-class gentrifiers understand the impact they are having, ten-year resident Mark Lewis told me:

> The artists/professional class [like me] are making it harder for the old Somerville folks to stay here, so there is sort of resentment when, say, grandma has been in an apartment for thirty years and all of a sudden has to move out because her rent went up . . . because all these people moved in . . . and it changes Somerville.

Mark was also concerned that, as areas such as Union Square become more attractive to more affluent residents, lower-income artists would be pushed out: "Artists move into a neighborhood, it becomes a desirable place to live, and then the artists can't afford to live there anymore. Young profession-als come in who make more money." His comment echoes the findings of urban studies scholars, who propose a "stage" model of gentrification, where increasingly affluent groups settle in a neighborhood at different points in time, beginning with less affluent artists and culminating with an highly affluent elite (Griffith 1995; Hannigan 1995).

Several people I interviewed talked about geographic divisions in Somer-ville that divide middle-class white newcomers from newcomers who are working-class immigrant people of color. Their comments reflect earlier reported facts that, in gentrified West Somerville, which includes the Davis Square area near Tufts University, only one-tenth of residents are non-white (Office of the Mayor 2008: 42), while in East Somerville, one-third are non-white and over one-fifth are Hispanic (OSPCD 2008: 196). As Kevin Brennan told me, "Somerville is becoming more and more segregated. . . . All the white kids live in West Somerville, all the black and Hispanic kids live in East Somerville. . . . [T]here's a cultural line east to west. West Somerville has become decreased in diversity." When I asked why this was occurring, Kevin said it was class that was causing this racial-ethnic divide, and he showed his own working-class perspective on middle-class newcomers: "Because minorities can't afford to live in West Somerville . . . there's a whole new upper middle class who's moved in . . . a kind of generic American where everyone's just the same." Peter Evans agreed that the city's class divide is geographical: "Really, Somerville is two towns. West Somerville has no affordable housing. . . . [I]f you try to do anything over there [to increase affordable housing], they're up in arms." These comments call to mind research showing that urban neighborhoods that claim to be cosmopolitan are actually often segregated by class and race (Lees 2008).

Acknowledged Benefits of Gentrification and a Common Vision for the City's Future

Various segments of Somerville's population are attracted to its demographic diversity and lively arts and restaurant scene. Angela DeLuca, a prominent member of the local business community and lifelong Somerville resident, is typical of someone who once considered moving to the suburbs but decided against it: "I don't want to drive an hour [to work]. I want to be close to the nightlife in Boston. I want to be close to the theater, the arts. I want to be close to the hospital." A house appraiser had told her: "The bloom is off the rose for suburbia. . . . People are moving back to the cities. People don't want to drive anymore. People don't want to move [to] the suburbs and be locked up in their house from Friday night to Sunday."

Another lifelong Somerville resident and prominent business leader, Bill Egan, told me:

> I have brothers and sisters who bought out in Tewksbury and Burlington, and now they would love to be back in the city . . . convenient to a Red Sox [baseball] game or to the symphony or wherever you want to go. You drive from Burlington, it's forty-five or fifty minutes, and you're getting toward ten, eleven o'clock at night.

The literature on new urban development and the "new urbanism" confirms this relatively recent focus on the appeal of life in city centers as areas for entertainment and consumption aimed largely at affluent populations (e.g., Strom 2008; Zukin 2009). Middle- and upper-middle-class people who can afford to live in the suburbs, like Angela DeLuca and Bill Eagan, may choose to live in smaller cities, such as Somerville, that are very close to major cities like Boston. They make this choice to avoid the time and effort it takes to maintain large suburban houses, care for big lawns, and make long commutes into the city. Rising fuel costs for cars and energy costs to heat and cool large suburban houses is another factor. Those who choose to live in cities also may feel alienated from what they experience as suburbia's isolation and homogeneous blandness.

It is not surprising that longtime Somerville residents, like Angela and Bill, who can afford the city's new amenities, find much to be pleased with about gentrification. What is surprising, given the potential negative effects of gentrification for older working-class residents, is that some of them also feel positively about Somerville's changes. This is consistent with research that argues that gentrification brings positive effects for older residents, even though it also threatens the ability of some to remain in the city (Freeman 2006; Sullivan 2007). Lifelong resident Adonia Xanthis said:

> All of a sudden, people want these old houses, which is kind of nice because twenty, twenty-five years ago, people didn't think there was any value to these very strong older houses. . . . So I'm glad people see the value of them. . . . I'm kind of sad that they've gotten so expensive that they have to condo-ize them. A two-family house that sells for $900,000, not many people can buy that. . . . But if you make it into two or three condos, people can buy them. Usually not families, so we've gotten away. . . . It was a very family-oriented city. . . . [Now] there's a lot of young, single people here, and that's kind of good too because it's a new perspective. . . . It's nice having a mixture. . . . When I was a kid, Davis Square was our hangout, and then Davis Square died. . . . Then all of a sudden it's very hip again, and I like that. I think it's really great. Other people are appreciating it. It's come to life.

Similar to Bill Egan and Angela DeLuca, Adonia said, "Everything is easy to get to. If I want to go to downtown Boston, I can get there in fifteen minutes, even with the bus or train. If I'm in the suburbs I can't do that."

Maria DeCosta, born and raised in Somerville and now well into her seventies, when asked about the best aspects of Somerville today, said, "Number

one is the great neighborhoods," and went on to name the features of gentrification in her neighborhood that she especially liked: "I love the new restaurants, all different kinds of ethnic restaurants. . . . We're going to have new
design in East Somerville to make it more walkable. . . . [W]e're going to get
pedestrian-friendly sidewalks and narrower roads and some beautification.
I'm looking forward to that." While concerned about the city's east-west
class and race divide, Maria also sees benefits to having middle-class gentrifiers in her east-side neighborhood: "The majority of professionals live in
West Somerville . . . but we're having, besides the immigrants moving into
the neighborhood, finally there is a mixture of professional people. It makes
people in the neighborhood happy that there is such a mix now." Maria also
said that having more middle-class people moving into Somerville improved
how others saw the city, alluding to the earlier characterization of "Slumerville": "[Before,] the reputation of the city was not very good and people
weren't moving in. The people who lived here were the people that lived here
for years and maybe didn't have any option but to stay [because they couldn't
afford to move]."

Prevailing discussions in the gentrification literature about class and race
conflict, and evidence from my research on those divisions in Somerville
would lead one to expect that Somerville's newer middle-class, mostly white,
professionals and newer working-class immigrant groups, made up of people of color, to hold different and contested visions for the future of their
city. However, that is not what I found. Instead, the civically engaged residents I talked with from all three segments of Somerville's population suggest more commonality than difference in how they see their city's current
assets and challenges, and in what they want their city to be like in the
future. People across class, race, and nationality as well as across the generations spoke to me with pride about Somerville's heritage as an immigrant
working-class city. People from the different segments of Somerville's populations told me how much they value the city's class, race, and ethnic diversity and said that this diversity is one of the reasons why they chose to make
their homes there and why they intend to stay. Lifelong residents (mainly
white ethnics) gave diversity as a reason to stay in the city where they were
born and raised. When I asked about the best aspects of living in Somerville,
Andrade Coelho, who was brought from the Azores as a young child over
half a century ago, said:

> I enjoy the cultural riches. It's important for me to see people who
> are brown, who are speaking different languages. I love going down
> to the Market Basket in Union Square. You're apt to hear thirty lan-

guages by the time you get to the checkout. . . . Ethiopian[s], Indians, Tibetans, Latinos. And the Latino groups come from El Salvador and Guatemala and Honduras. And then you'll hear Portuguese, but you hear Brazilian Portuguese. I enjoy that.

Sonia Pena, who is forty-six years of age, was born in Portugal, and has resided in Somerville since 1984, sees Somerville as "a good neighborhood. It's diverse. We have Portuguese, blacks, Italian[s], and Spanish people." Young Latino leader Jake Sanchez had a simple explanation for why he moved to the city ten years ago instead of to another nearby community: "[Somerville] just felt more racially mixed to me." Monique Clovet, who was born in Haiti and had been living in Somerville since 2000, said that the best thing about the city is this: "Our community and the diversity. Different languages, different shades. Listen to all the different voices. Imagine if we were all black or all white. Where would all the beauty and all the spices be?"

Vitor Branco, who was born in Brazil and has been living in Somerville for twenty years, said that the best thing about the city is that "Somerville is so diversified. It makes things easier for everybody. . . . I seen [sic] a lot of different cultures coming in the last ten to fifteen years. . . . You see a lot of Brazilian stores, bakeries . . . so many Brazilians here." Alberto Dias, who has lived in Somerville since 1980, told me he loves Somerville: "When I want an American restaurant, Mt. Vernon is there. When I want Italian, Vinny's is one of the best in the area. You want Mexican, you want Ethiopian, you want Salvadoran, you want Brazilian, Italian bakeries. They are all here."

The appeal of diversity in Somerville is not only a matter of ethnicity and race. It extends as well to class. Rosemary O'Hanrahan, a lifetime resident who is in her seventies, told me:

In Somerville, there's no class distinction in the sense that you can be a pauper or a king, or forgive me, a bookie, even—and you're treated the same. . . . Somerville has both rich and poor, but nobody's very rich. If somebody gets very rich, they move out. There is some poor, but it's [a] matter of degree. Pauper, prince, or cook, you're treated the same.

Adonia Xanthis, a lifelong Somerville resident and retired Somerville High School teacher, had a similar view: "I like Somerville because it's not a snobby place. That's one of my really important things that I like about it."

The class diversity in Somerville also appeals to those from the city's professional middle class, such as twenty-year resident Mike Kent. When I asked what he wants the city to be like in ten years, he responded: "I would like to see the city continue to have roughly the mix of people it has today, and that means that the lower-income cohorts would still have roughly comparable opportunities to be able to live here and thrive." Richard Strickland, who once headed a city department and who described himself as a "middle-class white guy," told me, "I don't want Somerville to be a suburb. . . . If there isn't room for people who are working class, then the tenor of life in the community is quite different." Peter Evans said succinctly, "I would like [Somerville] to be like it is, but only better." Like a number of others, Jake Sanchez offered relatively affluent West Somerville's Davis Square as an example of what he would not want for other areas of the city, like Union Square, saying, "I love Davis Square, but I couldn't afford a house within a mile of there, so I don't want every other square to become like that." Kevin Brennan said, "I would like to see the city remain affordable for people. I'd love to see a Somerville where people know their neighbors. . . . I still think it's the best place to live, and I wouldn't want to live anywhere else."

Somerville's diversity and concern about losing it to gentrification extend as well to its new, more recently arrived young professionals, such as arts leader Mark Lewis, who told me that he values the pride he hears expressed by longtime residents. "Davis Square," Mark also told me, "is maybe over the gentrified edge. . . . The ethnicity isn't as present. . . . It feels more ethnically white, whereas in Union Square, you feel the world coming together and I hope it keeps that." Peter Evans said, "We made a very conscious decision to live in a city . . . where you meet people with very different life histories and backgrounds. . . . I would go crazy living in the 'burbs, where everybody is like me." As Scott Mead said, comparing Somerville with a more affluent and less class- and race-diverse Boston area town, "If I wanted to live in Brookline, I'd live in Brookline."

Sheila Gayner, who bought a home in the city's east side ten years ago, also values the city's diversity, which she does not want to see altered: "[It's] a working-class city and an immigrant city, and it's also a city that is [an] urban, hip, interesting place to live for people who don't want to be surrounded by people who are exactly like themselves." About Somerville's next decade, she said:

> I don't want it to change much. I think the attraction to Somerville is that it is what it is. . . . The mix of the immigrants and the newcomers and the old-timers makes it a very interesting place to live. . . . I kind of would like it to stay to have that mix. I mean, I know the city

will change and I'm hoping to see some improvement, but I don't want it to lose its character.

Scott Mead, a local business leader who first moved to the city in the early 1990s and once ran for city alderman, had a similar view:

> I like the diversity. They always say [Somerville is] one-third immigrants, a third working class, a third yuppies that moved in, and all that push and pull and all is [a] microcosm [of] America, and it's wonderful. I think to lose that and have it become some yuppie town, [to have] working-class people get pushed out, [that would be] unfortunate.

Scott especially likes "the vibrancy. You walk down the street, and it's, 'Oh, how you doing?' You know people. . . . I like the close-knit feeling." So does Peter Evans, who said, "Somerville is [a] really dynamic place, a great artistic community, and lots of immigrants. . . . When you mix all these cultures together, you come up with just a really interesting result."

City Officials Caught in the Gentrification Dilemma and What It Means for Somerville's Future

Elected city officials consistently remark, both publicly and privately, about how much they, like the other city residents I talked with, value Somerville's diversity. In a typical comment, longtime "born and raised" resident Bruce Riley told me, "Diversity is what makes Somerville a great city." In addition to what city officials said in interviews, at public meetings, and in media reports, official city planning documents are consistently explicit about the commitment to preserving diversity and continuing to welcome newer immigrants and working-class and lower-income residents.

At the same time, elected officials also feel pressured by some older white ethnic constituents, who resist the presence of newer immigrant groups made up of people of color and resent the growing number of young middle-class professionals. These Somerville "old-timers" object to what they see as large numbers of "illegals," who in their view, consume the city's resources, threaten the city's safety, and take advantage of city services. City officials, including the immigrant-friendly mayor, are careful not to alienate these older, more conservative residents, who are known to vote in large numbers and who city officials make certain to get to the polls because they know they can count on their votes, in this city where a few hundred or fewer voters can decide elections. I considered this issue in Chapter 5 and discuss it further in Chapter 7.

Elected city officials also feel hard pressed to make resident displacement their number one priority, given Somerville's urgent need for new revenues from new affluent residents and new commercial businesses. As Peter Evans said, "The city's biggest problem is tax revenues. This is a very dependent city that desperately needs to cultivate a commercial tax base." Business leader Scott Mead told me: "You cannot run this city the way it's going. . . . We can't just keep putting it all on the residents. You need to get more of a commercial [tax] base. . . . So there's gotta be huge development."

Given this need, the major focus of official written city plans and frequent remarks by city officials at meetings I attended were often about how to attract new business and new, more affluent residents. New businesses (e.g., those planned for Assembly Square and Union Square) and more affluent residents to patronize them are expected to expand the city's tax base, which, it is generally agreed (among residents and city government alike) has long relied far too much on resident property taxes and too little on commercial taxes. A parallel emphasis by city officials on "quality of life" issues references city government's support of a lively arts and culture scene that includes summer street festivals and music events, plus new parks and an extended bicycle path aimed at attracting and keeping newer middle- and upper-class residents who can pay higher residential taxes.

It is of course true that some longtime residents of gentrifying cities such as Somerville see the rising costs of homes and new commercial development as an economic opportunity for themselves. Although I did not interview former residents who had taken advantage of the rising real estate values to sell their Somerville houses for considerable sums of money, a few people I talked with told me about them. The opportunity to make money from Somerville redevelopment projects and the resulting gentrification also came up when I asked a longtime elected city official why nearly all of the aldermen had showed up for the ward meeting in East Somerville when they usually attend only the meeting in their own ward:

> A lot of us want to make sure we're on top of any changes. . . . I tell my people my advice is that if you want to buy any property, buy it now in [East Somerville] because all of [the main street] is going to be redone, and Assembly Square is under construction now. IKEA is going to open soon. . . . It's going to be a very popular place, with the new Orange Line station being built. People are going to flock

there. . . . We're changing the gateway into the city from [from Boston, and so] East Somerville is going to be a good place to be, a real magnet.

In summary, it is important not to overstate my claim of a shared vision among the three main segments of Somerville's population for the future of this changing city. Even if it is as present as my interviews suggest, this vision alone, of course, is not going to prevent the displacement of working-class and/or immigrant residents. However, such a shared vision could potentially provide a foundation to mobilize city residents from all three of Somerville's main population groups to support affordable housing and other measures aimed at preventing displacement. Such an alliance would admittedly be difficult to build and sustain, and as business leader Scott Mead told me, "It's going to be extremely challenging when the Green Line comes in. . . . I think the rents are going to go through the roof, and it's probably a lost cause and that's a shame." As Peter Evans said, "There are still a lot of ways Somerville could go wrong."

What actions might avert what Scott Mead reluctantly sees as a lost cause and Peter Evans sees as the dangers of going wrong? A constituency base for anti-displacement measures could arise from a collaboration of the two populations that are most threatened. These groups are the working-class, often older, white ethnics and the newer, typically working-class, non-white immigrants. A shared class position could be a bridge, a unifier, between these two groups. However, I saw little evidence of these two groups joining during the time of my research, and other research has found that building this kind of alliance is extremely difficult, given racism and the unwillingness of older white ethnics to share power with newer, non-white immigrants (Betancur 2002). Still, both the Affordable Housing Organizing Committee and East Somerville Neighbors for Change, discussed in Chapter 3, have been somewhat successful in incorporating people from these two very different populations and placing them in positions of leadership. Along with progressive members of the city's growing middle class, they are working together toward common goals of anti-displacement. There have been and likely will continue to be disagreements in Somerville over development-related issues, such as how high new buildings should be, what portion of new housing should be reserved as affordable, where the new Green Line subway stops should be, and how much open space should be created. Pressures that the city feels to achieve "value-enhancing investments" (Bentacur 2002: 802) may indeed pose the greatest threat to Somerville's working-class and immigrant heritage.

However, the more basic underlying struggle in Somerville today is, at its root, not about gentrification or displacement, although it is often played out around those very real issues. The deeper struggle is over local power more generally, about who the city's elected officials will be and how they will govern. That struggle is going on between the city's newcomers and longtime city residents who occupy the major base of power in city government. This topic is the focus of Chapter 7.

7

Extending Social Citizenship, Remaking City Governance

> Despite our relative peace, we live with a persistent undercurrent of tension—Between those who have lived here all their lives and those who are new; Between those born in this country and those who are recent immigrants; Between those who can afford rising housing costs and those who are just getting by; Between those who seek immediate action on development issues and those who seek a different vision. (Curtatone 2004)

The passage from the mayor of Somerville's January 2004 inaugural speech, which also opens this book, is an eloquent expression of the social divisions in the city. They are the same divisions that this book has explored and that I have characterized as separating those who enjoy full community membership (social citizenship) from those who do not. Those groups with a greater measure of social citizenship in Somerville (and likely in other cities and towns around the United States) belong to the first groups in the mayor's paired list: lifelong "born and raised" city residents versus those who have come more recently, the native born versus the foreign born, middle-class versus low-income residents, city leaders who want to make fast decisions versus engaged residents who want a more participatory democratic process that I have called shared governance.

This final chapter describes both how Somerville's political "old guard" has managed thus far to hold back changes in who is elected to city government and how newer forces in the city are trying to make exactly that change.

This chapter also summarizes what I found in answer to the main research question that prompted this book: What conditions and circumstances facilitate civic and political engagement in the public life of this urban community? I conclude the book by returning to larger questions about the role of community voluntary associations in relation to government and about the incorporation (social citizenship) of new immigrants in regard to democratic shared governance.

Middle-class activist and twenty-year Somerville resident Peter Evans spoke pointedly about who has political power in Somerville:

> I think it's probably generally accepted that the traditional Irish and Italian immigrants here sort of dominate city politics. . . . The older folks vote a lot more than the new folks, especially more than the new immigrants. So when they shuttle people out of elderly housing for election day, it's who you grew up with and who you knew . . . and that's a huge part of city politics. . . . It's really hard for newcomers, and this is not just immigrants; it's young professionals and other types of people who come into the city. It's very hard for them to be represented because of the power structure, which is pretty much looking back a few generations to the people who were here in the forties and fifties. . . . I can think of only one alderman who isn't part of that.

As I have shown in previous chapters, issues of redevelopment, gentrification, resident displacement, and periodic events that threaten the immediate safety and security of Somerville's newer immigrants all provide important opportunities for civic and political engagement. They are also the issues and events that bring to the surface what I see as the central underlying struggle in the city today. That struggle, expressed earlier by Peter Evans, is about more than these issues or events. At a deeper level, it is about who governs this city and how they govern. In other words, it is a struggle for local power between those "born and raised," largely Irish and Italian, "old guard," working-class residents who have held power for over fifty years and those who live in the city that the old guard considers newcomers. These "newcomers" are immigrants, largely Brazilians, Latinos, and Haitians, plus white Anglo middle-class professionals. Many have lived in this city for twenty years or more. In addition to being a struggle for local power, what is occurring in Somerville today is a struggle for democracy, for what young Latino leader Jake Sanchez calls "open transparent government," for which, he says, "you've got to have the immigrants at the table, you've got to have the young, new, middle-class families who have moved here at the table."

The Missing in Somerville City Government

This book is about a city deservedly celebrated for its high degree of civic and political engagement. However, what is missing is a well-organized collective effort across race and class to remake city government so that elected officials are representative of the city's diverse constituencies. How the city is governed is also a point of contention, although active residents acknowledge that the current city administration, in place since 2004, has increased transparency and openness compared with previous administrations. Ted Nolan, for example, praised the city's relatively new mayor-appointed community development director "as open and inclusive a department leader as I could imagine. . . . She's doing a great job trying to include different voices from the community." Quoting members of the city's progressive Democrats, a local newspaper offered kudos to the city administration for holding open public discussions about the city's budget (Guha 2009b).

At the same time, immigrant leader Vertus Bernique, a resident for over two decades, offered an analysis of the city's political power structure that was very similar to that of white middle-class "newcomer" Peter Evans, quoted earlier. Vertus told me:

> What I see in Somerville is an old boy city. Things are not transparent. It's about how well connected you are. People will say, "Oh, they are the ones born and raised in Winter Hill," even when they're not. The decision making is from the people who were born here, and the father and the grandfather. . . . Even [when] their parents are from another country, they feel they have ownership of the city. Those are the people who are running the city.

Juliana Silva, an immigrant leader who has lived in the city for fifteen years, spoke similarly, "It's still the old boys, old school. We don't have anyone of color in government." Young Latino leader Jake Sanchez saw the same:

> The people who run our government don't reflect who lives in our city, and that's a problem. You can walk into City Hall, you can walk into a Board of Aldermen meeting or a School Committee meeting, and you don't see the diversity of races or ethnic backgrounds or even the folks who've been here less than ten years who've been involved and invested in the community, the younger folks. So how do we really engage and have true civic participation of everyone, not just lifelong residents? That's the challenge.

While newer immigrant groups are the ones most absent from positions in city government, "new" middle-class professionals also experience relative absence. Dave Strong, a city activist involved with city government for decades, told how he still feels like an outsider alongside Somerville old-timers: "It's still true [that] if you go to community meetings, a lot of people will describe themselves as a lifelong Somerville resident. I don't know if it's intentionally to make people feel who didn't grow up here that they're at a disadvantage, but that's always been my impression."

When I asked what changes they would like to see, immigrant leaders such as Vertus Bernique were quick to answer:

> I'd like to see the city be more inclusive because although I've been saying there's a lot of progress, look at who's in the leadership, all the heads of departments. I don't see any immigrants whatsoever. I don't see my community. I don't see the Latin community. So we're still basically on the outside. . . . I know it takes time and commitment, but it can happen.

Juliana Silva agreed:

> First we need to hire representatives of color in city government. . . . The mayor, his family barely spoke English, but he's also buddies with the old-timers. We cannot elect anyone new in City Hall and he supports the old-timers, and it gets so ugly. . . . I think the mayor needs to be more adventuresome about what it is to be an immigrant, him being first generation. It's okay if you lose support on one side. You're going to get it on the other. He's well seen by all the immigrant groups.

As I said, Somerville's newer middle-class professional residents have made somewhat greater inroads into elected office compared with newer immigrant groups. Dave Strong told me:

> Even though, ten or twelve years ago, you had a large population of educated middle-class professionals, they were not very involved in the community and they really didn't have much influence. Now the numbers are so large and a lot of professional people have been here for quite a while . . . they have a lot of influence. The current mayor understands this.

When I asked Juliana Silva why middle-class professionals have been more successful than immigrant groups at gaining access, she said:

> It's the power of being middle class, [being] computer savvy, knowing how to advocate for yourself and your needs, having a sense of community organizing, coming from a family where probably parents were involved in the school. . . . They meet with the mayor, they ask, they know how to lobby. Where immigrants, you know, it's being powerless [and] very humble.

Peter Evans agreed with Juliana, when he said of people like himself: "They know the system. They know what's possible. . . . If you're someone like me, a white guy who speaks English with a college education, it's very easy to get involved. . . . It's really hard if you're not a native English speaker." As Sandra Leavey, another middle-class professional, put it, "Class and language. Those are the big dividers [in this city]."[1]

As discussed earlier, an objective perusal of who actually occupies elected positions confirms the homogeneity that people I interviewed described. The office of the mayor has been occupied for over fifty years by men (and one woman) of either Irish or Italian heritage. Only one person of another ethnic group (a man of Portuguese descent) is remembered as having run for mayor during all that time. As of 2012, not a single person of Latino, Brazilian, Haitian, or Asian heritage was on the city's eleven-member Board of Aldermen. One alderman, a young, white, progressive woman, is from the city's growing class of young, middle class professionals. A 2009 campaign for alderman by an established Latino leader who has lived in the city for thirty years, a 2007 campaign for alderman by a young Latino leader, and another campaign for School Committee several years ago by a Haitian man all ended in failure. The 2007 campaign I describe in Chapter 2 turned ugly when, the day before the election, supporters of the longtime incumbent circulated a photo of the Latino candidate (in what was clearly a digitalized image) smiling down at a large, threatening-looking, dark-skinned teenage male wearing a hooded sweatshirt. The caption said that the candidate had opposed the Gang Ordinance, thus hampering police efforts to curb violence in the city, and also said that he had "welcomed" a local gang member into a city youth program. According to one of the city's main newspapers, seven thousand of these provocative flyers were mailed to (among other locales) the city's elderly housing developments, playing directly into older, heavily voting residents' fears about Latino gangs in the city (Editorial 2007).

The city's elected School Committee has historically been a path to subsequent election to the Board of Aldermen, but the School Committee, like the Board of Aldermen currently, has not one member who is Latino, Brazilian, Haitian, or Asian. One woman of Portuguese heritage has served on the School Committee for a number of years. The city's middle-class white residents have done better, as of 2011 claiming four of the nine School Committee seats.

A Political Old Guard Holding On to Power

One of the ways people told me that longtime elected Somerville officials keep their place is political patronage, even though all agreed that this has declined in recent years. Sam Martin, a prominent local activist for three decades, described what he called Somerville's "working-class politics left over from the old days." He saw these as modeled after the way in which Boston's Irish took over that city from its long-standing Yankee elite:

> Here's a story that captures it. When I first started to do community projects in Somerville, I sat at a desk in the mayor's office of services . . . next to a woman who . . . had a picture on her desk of over a hundred people [taken at her sixtieth birthday party], with nobody more distantly related than a third cousin. There was a Somerville cop, a water department employee, an employee of the electrical lines, etc., etc. This was how the political establishment in Somerville stayed in power . . . huge Irish families, and after all the intermarriage, you have hundreds of votes, all living in the city. All you have to do is give a job to four or five of those people, and whoever the mayor is who gave them the job gets all of their votes as mayor or alderman or whatever. . . . You had to be very careful what you said about anybody because the likelihood was that they were somebody's cousin or aunt or sister-in-law. . . . So this is how power is maintained, through the patronage system, with aldermen who have four brothers who all have city jobs.[2]

High-profile local activist Sheila Gayner, who is a middle-class professional, made the same point succinctly: "It's all about jobs. You know, if your relative has a job because of an elected official, you're loyal to that elected official. So whether that elected official is doing good things for the community or not, they have your loyalty." Dave Strong agreed:

Somerville has a municipal government that's somewhat of a typical municipal machine. Every mayor uses the city apparatus for patronage to give jobs to their supporters. That's just the way cities tend to work. . . . People still get jobs because of who they know. . . . Jobs hit people's pocketbooks and determine their lives, and then they're eternally grateful to you.

Residents who are concerned about the absence of newer immigrant groups in city elected posts are frustrated because, as they see it, longtime city officials have too often failed to institute new policies and practices that could facilitate immigrant political incorporation. Based on public forums I attended where these old-timers spoke out and quotes by those officials that I read in local newspapers, the frustration of the residents I talked with was well grounded. At the time of my study, the following reforms had not been instituted: routine language translation at city meetings, regular printing of city documents and public announcements over the city's call system in multiple languages, routine voter registration drives in immigrant neighborhoods, multi-lingual ballots, and extension of the vote in local elections to non-citizens. In Chapter 5, I discuss the refusal by a majority of the city's Board of Aldermen to sign on to the Welcoming Somerville initiative, even though it had been readily endorsed by the mayor and the city's elected School Committee.

While most of those I interviewed spoke well of the city's young, reform-minded mayor, immigrant leaders and their allies and advocates wanted him to take stronger action to institute new governing practices and support new political leadership. Alvarado Marquez told me that the mayor withheld active support for these kinds of reform measures because he had to retain the loyalty of longtime elected officials to continue to win elections. If the mayor went too far in helping newcomers to gain political office, Alvarado explained, the "old guard" would mobilize their older, dependable, "born and raised" voting blocs and simply vote him out of office. Indeed, as I was told, it is only because the mayor continues to lend his support to the city's longest-serving aldermen that he can at the same time sign on to immigrant-friendly initiatives, such as the Welcoming Somerville campaign, and to make statements, like the oft-quoted "Everybody is welcome in Somerville. . . . I don't care what your [immigration] status is," and still keep his place as mayor. As long as he remained otherwise loyal, Marquez and others explained to me, the mayor was able to advocate for some issues that the old-timers disagreed with.

When I asked Juliana Silva why city officials resisted active reforms that could increase immigrant participation in local politics, the answer I got was simple and clear: "People are afraid . . . of losing their seats." As Sam Martin put it, "They don't want to relinquish power." Referring to the flyer that circulated when pre-election polls in 2007 showed a win for the Latino challenger, Sam said, "They really fight, and it's a very unpleasant and dirty politics."[3]

Those elected officials I interviewed who belong to the city's political "old guard" told me that the city was heavily involved in offering services to welcome new immigrants into the community. Longtime alderman Bruce Riley, born in the city over fifty years ago and residing there ever since, said: "The leaders of the city are very welcoming, [and] there are a lot of programs in place to welcome the new immigrant." Longtime Somerville city officials see the challenge of immigrant incorporation into local politics not in structural or institutional terms, but rather in individual terms. When I asked them why immigrants are not more politically engaged, I heard that immigrants should "just get involved," take an active interest, become informed. Eventually, these "newcomers" would "just naturally" begin to ascend to elected posts in city government, just as these leaders' Irish and then Italian ancestors had done long ago in the face of Yankee domination. Recall longtime incumbent alderman Sean Russo, who told me: "If you want to have influence in this city, register, vote, and participate. In my ward, I could probably give you the name[s] of 150 people that I know I'm going to talk with when I'm up for reelection, and those 150 can swing me easily."[4] Russo took the view that a change in who led city politics would come with time.[5]

Riley also told me that he had been involved in "not too successful" voter registration drives focused on immigrants. In his experience, immigrant residents (and, to some extent, younger, middle-class professional newcomers) were simply not as interested in running for public office as were members of his own generation:

> It takes a lot of money and a lot of hard work to beat an incumbent. . . . Half the city is probably old-time Somerville, people who have always lived here. Maybe the other half moved in over the last thirty or forty years. But those 50 percent of people who have lived here vote to put people in office . . . so the people who grew up here . . . have an advantage. [They tell the voters,] "You know my brothers and sisters." "You know me." "I was your altar boy." "I was your paperboy."

Prominent businessman and lifelong resident Bill Egan shared Riley's view of who the active voters are in city elections: "When you look at the demographics of who's voting in Somerville, it's . . . people that have been here forever. It's the seniors. Seniors' vote is huge, and people like me vote big." Dick O'Neil described how he holds on to his alderman seat by emphasizing his hometown credentials to these voters: "I say, 'Listen, I've lived in the city. I'm a native guy. I'm a Somerville native. I've been here. . . . I'm the member with the most experience.'"

It would be a mistake to claim that members of Somerville's political old guard are either unaware of or uninterested in the circumstances—racial, linguistic, and economic—of their Brazilian, Latino, Haitian, or other immigrant constituents. Indeed, one way that these elected officials hold on to their power is by providing individual help of various kinds to people from the immigrant community, while at the same time not supporting measures that could advance that community in political terms. A prominent immigrant leader I interviewed for this study told about a longtime city alderman who "refused to have a conversation about what it is to be undocumented," despite repeated invitations to do so. On the other hand, when I asked immigrant leader Monique Clovet about her own longtime elected city representative, she offered a somewhat tight-lipped reply:

> I have no complaints about him. If I have any problem, I call him. I say, "Can you please send someone over to shovel the street and put some salt on it?" And he's always there. He always return [sic] my calls. Not too many people would like to hear what I have to say [about him], but based on my experience, I have no problem with him.

Part of what was also interesting about both Russo and Riley is that, while they were not willing to support active policies and practices that could ease immigrants into political participation and elected office, they were not blind to the overt racism that sometimes faced newer immigrants of color in the city. Both men spoke spontaneously about what Russo pejoratively called the city's "white establishment" and what Riley recognized as residents who do not welcome new residents of color. In other words, Riley stated, "I think there are a lot of individuals who live in the city who aren't as welcoming [as we leaders are]. I get calls [from constituents] complaining about black families [that] I don't get about white families."

Unlike some members of the city's political old guard, many of the actively engaged residents I talked with understood that, when a sizable segment of a city's population is entirely missing from political representation and from significant levels of political participation, both democracy and diversity are weakened. As community leader Mike Kent told me:

> Some of the answers I seek for Somerville in terms of wanting to sustain a kind of diversity that we have today . . . do really depend on . . . newcomer populations amass[ing] enough power that their voices get strong enough that they begin to be represented. I do think it has to be represented in the halls of government at some point. Otherwise, the voice just isn't there."

Challenging and Defending an Entrenched Power Structure: Progressive versus Traditional Democrats

In Somerville, membership in the Democratic Party is virtually universal. The traditional wing of the party is understood to represent the older, working-class population that is largely of Irish and Italian heritage. The Progressive Democrats of Somerville (PDSers) represent progressive members of the new and growing middle class and, to a lesser extent, newer immigrants. Greater Boston's main newspaper described these groups:

> Two factions have long vied for power in this densely packed city, where sharp elbows are more than occasionally thrown in. The groups are defined broadly as the "old guard" consisting of lifelong residents, lunch-bucket Democrats . . . and the "reformists," who draw heavily from the ranks of liberal-leaning activists who have been migrating to Somerville for decades and whose numbers have swelled in recent years. (Jonas 2008)

The main goals of the PDSers are more diverse political representation (social citizenship) and greater transparency and participation in public decision making (shared governance). Jake Sanchez told me, "Our motto is 'Democracy Demands Participation.'" As newcomer resident Ted Nolan, a progressive-identified professional who once ran (unsuccessfully) for city alderman, said, "I'd like to see a government that felt more inclusive and transparent about what's going on. I think there's still a little too much 'we'll take care of it' kind of politics in Somerville." Illustrating the connection that the PDSers see between immigrant political incorporation (an aspect of what I call here social citizenship) and some form of shared governance, one (also unsuccessful) candidate in the city's 2008 election who was endorsed by the PDS wrote in his statement to the group: "Progress is about . . . working to build a stronger, more inclusive and transparent democratic process. In Somerville, this means bring[ing] more new immigrants and people of color into local government and politics."

The division between traditional and progressive Democrats in Somerville, I was told, is a bitter one. Dave Strong, a progressive and a twenty-year resident, described it as a "struggle for control . . . where the [local] politics' tectonic plates meet, two big forces, the progressives and the traditionals." When I asked Bruce Riley, from the "traditional" wing of the party, a general question about what conflicts he saw in the city, he said without hesitation, "Well, you have the Progressive Democrats, and you've got the Democratic Party Committee. And even though they both claim they are fighting for the same causes, they are both registering Democrats and trying to put Democrats into office, there is tension between these two groups." When I asked what issues they disagree about, he laughed and said, "Every issue." When I pressed further, he said, "You know the [establishment local newspaper] has their little 'News Talk,' and it says that of the three contested races, this is who the Progressive Democrats are looking to endorse. . . . I'm sure if anyone ran against me, they would probably endorse my opponent." Another longtime city alderman, Dick O'Neil, noted this same conflict between old and new Democrats. When I asked him the same question about the issues of disagreement, he too laughed and said, "Everything!" When I pressed him about the difference between himself and the "progressives," he acknowledged that the differences were "philosophical," and he characterized the self-identified Somerville progressives as "elitist."

Residents from the city's progressive Democrat organization also talked about the contested relationship between themselves and the city's political old guard. Deb Morris, a young newcomer in city affairs who quickly became a PDS leader, said, "There's a huge conflict between political newcomers and political old-timers. They just don't like each other. They get in [to] verbal fights. . . . I don't know what the issues are, really. . . . I think a lot of it is . . . territorial, like you're coming [into] my city."[6] When I asked Jake Sanchez about the issues on which the two groups disagreed, he said, "It's more about process than outcome. They're more to do with how decisions get made, how inclusive, how transparent. . . . We want to bring all the groups to the table." Sanchez told me that before progressive residents formally organized into the PDS, more of the older Somerville residents identified as politically liberal or progressive. However, once the PDS became a visible force in the city, then the old-timers unified against what they saw as intruding newcomers. This history suggests that their conflict is about the old-timers versus the new people, consistent with this chapter's opening quotation by the city's newly inaugurated mayor in 2004.

When I asked progressives to tell me what those in elected positions of power in the city actually did to put up barriers to newcomers, one person told me, "The city makes it very difficult to get involved if you disagree with what they see as the right approach." On one occasion, the mayor reportedly raised a question about someone a local community organization had nominated (at the mayor's request) for a citywide committee. This was given to me as an example of "what the city does to push back. It forces people to jump through a hoop, to feel maybe not as wanted [if they're politically active people] who may raise tough questions and maybe not always support what the city power structure wants. It's not specific to this mayor. It's the structure. Either you're on board or you're not." I was also told about the mayor's reported habit of personally telephoning members of progressive activist groups who were working on some issue and "telling them they needed to back off." According to one person who told me this story, it shows how the city's powerful political figures exclude new voices from becoming involved in city decision making: "Instead of bringing them into the conversation and encouraging them to be part of it, they're seen as people [who are] not on the same page, so [the city] is going to push those people back. . . . I think the city puts up barriers to people [who are] not born and raised in this community to being involved, and that's a real struggle."

Others alluded to how longtime Somerville "pols" appeal to what I describe in Chapter 5 as a working-class "imaginary" to connect to the city's main voting bloc by claiming a working-class identity. As middle-class newcomer Peter Evans explained, "I think politicians like to think of Somerville as a working-class city." As one relatively new local political activist told me, "Somerville . . . doesn't want to be the People's Republic of Cambridge." This refers to a pejorative label used to exaggerate the political liberalism of relatively affluent Cambridge, Massachusetts, which borders on less affluent Somerville. As Sanchez also explained:

> [In Somerville,] we want to be more blue collar,[7] more hard nosed. . . .
> So there's a protectiveness about what Somerville believes it is, and
> when new people come in you're always questioned about your motives and how long you've been here. . . . People at community meetings I go to will often say they've lived here their whole lives, and I used to wonder why they were saying that. People tell me I've only lived here since yesterday, even though I've done a lot of work in the city.

When I asked people about the PDSers' accomplishments, I heard about successes in getting at least a few new people, "not the usual players," to run for office.[8] At the same time, progressive activists from Somerville's newer professional middle class also recognized that they have not worked hard enough to bring in segments of Somerville's older residents who would likely support the PDS agenda. This book has quoted individuals from Somerville's working-class, white, ethnic population "born and raised" in Somerville, such as Maria DeCosta, who would likely agree with much of the PDS agenda but who are not involved in the organization. As Sanchez told me, "We haven't done enough to connect with old-time Somerville residents who may share our views, especially those that are low income. We liberals also haven't done enough to connect to the newer immigrant groups in the city." I consider this further later.

Change in the Who and How of Local Politics?

Prominent business owner and lifelong Somerville resident Bill Egan took the view that the potential for newer immigrant groups to gain power in the city was substantial: "I think that an immigrant [running for office] would have a pretty good shot because they have a pretty good constituency . . . especially now, where you have the larger groups . . . . Say you had a Brazilian candidate. There are a lot of Brazilians in Somerville." Dave Strong thinks that some amount of change is already evident: "I'd say the folks who have ultimate power are from pretty much the same group, but I think there's people [in appointed positions] that didn't grow up here. This mayor has brought in a lot of people from the outside." Sheila Gayner agreed with Strong that change in who ran the city was happening, albeit slowly: "Transitions are happening. . . . But it's not happening quickly, and to be honest with you, whoever the elected officials are who can get the senior vote, they are the ones who win."

Dave Strong also noted that several relatively recently elected individuals who represent Somerville in the state legislature are, unlike city officials, not members of the city's "born and raised" old guard but rather are younger progressives. The process that creates this situation offers another opportunity for future change in who governs Somerville. He explained how the same population of voters could elect such different candidates for local versus state office:

> [It's about] odd versus even years of election. A lot more people come out to vote in even years, when you have state office [elections]. In

odd years, when you only have municipal elections, a lot fewer people come out to vote and it's predominantly people who grew up here
or who've lived here a long time and are connected, so that's why
getting elected to state rep is very different from getting elected to a
municipal position.

I asked him to explain more about who voted in city elections and why:

The point is the old pols have a limited number of people they can
get out. In [state election] years, everyone comes out, and they're not
[all] connected to people who grew up here and they don't have the
same sense of politics that what I call the lunch bucket Democrats
do. They're more likely to vote progressive. [But] a lot of those folks
don't come out to vote in municipal elections.

One does not have to be a wise political pundit to notice that relying on
"the senior vote" is not a long-term strategy for retaining political power.
While natural attrition will eventually bring about change in Somerville's
elected officials, a number of possibilities and conditions exist for a more
active and, ideally, less slow approach to moving the city's Brazilians, Latinos, Haitians, and other immigrant groups into office. Some are the same
conditions and circumstances that support the overall relatively high level of
civic and political engagement in this All-America City.

One factor is the potential for joining as political allies the city's two
"newcomer" groups, uniting the city's growing white middle class with its
immigrants. A shared vision for the city's future across social divides, discussed in Chapter 6, supports this potential. Another is Somerville's tendency toward a politics that is contentious yet collegial, "hot" yet quick to
cool, occurring within the context of a medium-size, densely populated
city, where people who are active in public affairs are likely to know each
other. This is accompanied by a hands-on, if-I-don't-do-it-no-one-else-will,
fight-for-everything approach to political activity (and to life in general). Yet
another is the presence of numerous visible and active voluntary associations
discussed throughout this book. Next I look more closely at each of these circumstances and possibilities for political change.

In terms of connecting the two different "newcomer" groups to act
together politically to change the face of elected officials, like a number of
others I spoke with, middle-class resident Sheila Gayner, a highly engaged
"newcomer," sees these divides as beginning to fade:

> When I first moved here [in 1999], it seemed much more divisive. I mean, I think it's still divisive, but I think there was super hostility to newcomers, particularly progressives, thinking they wanted to turn the city into something else. And the fact is, I think a lot of people are on the same side, but the way they describe things are different. They want the same things.

Jake Sanchez makes the point that the two "newcomer" groups especially have much in common in terms of wanting to remake local government, a commonality that provides a basis for bringing them together politically: "Newer [middle-class] folks and the progressive folks, their natural allies are the immigrants, not ideologically always . . . but there are more similarities than differences. We all want a more open government that gives more voice to more people, opportunities for different people to get involved."

In regard to Somerville's tendency toward action, some people spoke to me about a culture in the city emphasizing just making things happen. As Sally Campo, a resident activist for three decades, explained it: "Somerville is a working-class community, and I don't think people are afraid of getting their hands dirty, and that has supported people just jumping in and getting whatever needs doing done. I grew up that way too. If you wanted it done, you did it. I found that Somerville had that." This capacity for doing it yourself and not expecting someone else to do it is supported by the city's size and density: "[Somerville isn't] so big that you couldn't imagine you could make a difference, four square miles. . . . Just a few people can make a difference. . . . From a strong social capital perspective, there's a lot of interweaving and people knowing each other." A number of those I talked with and heard speak at community meetings expressed appreciation, pride, and pleasure in a combative yet collegial approach to Somerville politics. Local business leader Scott Mead, for example, told me, when I asked him what he thought were the best things about Somerville: "I like the people. I like that, even when you get into this big knock-down drag out fight in a community meeting, I see [the participants] walking around town later and we say hi and it's not personal. . . . You get into everything, you duke it out, and when it's over, you shake hands . . . and I think that's great."

Local news reports from which I have quoted in previous chapters also referred to Somerville's tolerance for conflict and for hashing out disagreements in a direct and forthright manner and then being able to go on as before. It is worth considering that this tendency could be necessary for a highly engaged form of democracy. As Campo suggested, it may be connected to the city's relatively small size and high level of density, which creates a context for closer, more informal, and more intense relationship. As Campo also suggested, it may also be rooted in the working-class culture that many Somervillians claim.

The presence of active civil society organizations with the potential for connecting the city's social divides also carries the possibility for collective political action that could change the who and how of politics in Somerville. The role of these organizations is especially important for non-citizens "who cannot directly access the political system through their votes" (Ramakrishnan and Bloemraad 2008a: 31). I discuss in Chapter 3 the community coalition of associations that designed and conducted a highly inclusive decision-making process for creating a vision for the city's future, a process that ran in parallel with (but separate from) the city's "official" visioning process. Indicating that city officials had heard and responded to this call for democratic participation in planning for the city's future, officials subsequently agreed not to proceed with further planning around major redevelopment sites until residents had had multiple opportunities to take an active part in the citywide community visioning process (Guha 2009a). This kind of engaged process for public decision making carries a strong possibility for helping to create change in both the who and how of local governance.

In discussing how community organizations can work together to create change, middle-class professional Sally Campo, a thirty-year resident and activist, saw some movement toward greater shared activism around immigrant issues among some local nonprofit organizations:

> I've seen some good work happening around the mobilization of SCC [Somerville Community Corps] and CAAS [Community Action Agency of Somerville] and the Welcome Project on some joint issues, like in-state tuition [for non-citizens]. . . . We can think and act together and align with regional and statewide initiatives because the Somerville organizations don't have the clout to do things independently.

Civil society organizations in Somerville, then, do help to connect people across the social divides that the mayor described at the beginning of this chapter, and they often work together to improve the lives of newer immigrants. However, with regard to actually mobilizing the city's newer immigrants and their allies to become active participants in political processes and to remake city government, several of those I talked with saw substantial limitations of local nonprofits (as opposed to voluntary associations) in mobilizing against the city's current political old guard. Steve Smith expressed his view that even community organizations like his, which advocated for local immigrants, most likely would not become effective agents of political change because, in his view, "nonprofits are by definition highly particular service-based groups":

> There's a housing one, a homelessness one, a youth group. . . . They meet together, but they don't have a common agenda. No one is against anyone else's agenda but they also are all competing for the same scarce public and foundation resources, so I don't think the whole is going to sum up into some larger change agent.

Sam Martin, well-known local immigrant advocate, took a similar tack, saying, "At the moment, I don't really see it pulling together and working. . . . Nonprofits can't confront the city because they have to do business with them." Latino activist Alvarado Marquez expressed a view common in nonprofit literature (Immergluck 2005): "Nonprofits . . . a lot of them get funding through the city so they don't want to say anything against the city." Other research also suggests that nonprofits fear reprisal if they are suspected of violating Internal Revenue Service rules that limit their political activities (Berry 2003).

Jake Sanchez contrasted Somerville nonprofits with those in Boston proper, saying:

> In Boston, [community nonprofits] push the envelope in terms of advocacy and political involvement in a way that Somerville groups do not. Like [Somerville's community development agency that] can push the city, but relies heavily on the city to support housing development. If [that agency] does something the city doesn't like, it has happened, they call [the director] in and read him the riot act and say next time maybe we won't work with you. That can happen in Boston too, but Boston is much bigger, so there are more people to bring together [to challenge the city].

Other research shows that when these organizations are racially and ethnically representative of local constituencies, they are more likely to actively mobilize constituencies for political action (LeRoux 2009). This suggests the extreme importance for Somerville community nonprofits to become more diversified in terms of inclusion of newer immigrant groups, a project that organizations in the city have taken on, to greater and lesser degrees of success.[9]

While factors like those identified earlier do offer possibilities for political change in Somerville, what is currently absent is a clear, sustained, organized effort to bring the city's diverse groups of immigrants together, support people from those groups in running for election, and get them and their allies out to vote. Making political change of this kind will require figuring out ways to work more effectively together across local divides of class, race, ethnicity, language, and national origin—a challenge widely discussed and acknowledged in the city, but as yet largely unmet. It will require creating common agendas, building new leadership, and acting politically in concert in a way that everyone I talked with agreed is not occurring now. This is a challenge for making connections not only between old and new residents but also among the multiple groups of newer immigrants, who represent different nationalities, speak different languages, and come from very different cultures. As longtime Somerville immigrant leader Vertus Bernique said, "In terms of any of these communities really integrating with each other, it's not happening. . . . So, basically, we do our thing separately." Bill Egan, whose quote at the beginning of this section expressed optimism about Somerville's large immigrant constituency electing one of their own to political office, said, "It's organizing to get them out and to work for their candidate. . . . I'm not seeing that on any large scale." Steve Smith said that while local immigrant groups lack influence in the city, "They're very well organized in terms of religious activity and at certain times entrepreneurial activity and cultural activity, but not politics."

Like most of those I spoke with, Sam Martin believes that the only way that the newer immigrants will ever gain power is through directly seeking and winning elected positions in local government. Deb Morris, a young resident newcomer who heads a small local nonprofit and is active in the city's progressive political group, was a bit more positive about what she thought nonprofits could do politically—but for her, as for others, entering politics directly was what was necessary for the city's new middle-class and immigrant groups to gain power. As she put it, "Our nonprofit has done a lot of work creating relationships with the city so we can get things done. So, although we do have a voice, elected officials have a bigger one."

Conclusion

This book has told a story of a rapidly changing urban community that was nationally recognized as an All-America City for its high level of civic and political engagement. This story is about opposition and collaboration, division and unity. It is about a community composed of an old, white, ethnic working class that still runs the city alongside two populations of relative newcomers who bring class and racial-ethnic diversity to the city. Many of the so-called newcomers have lived in the city since the 1980s. While active in community affairs, they are still almost entirely absent from elected positions in city government. This results in an ongoing struggle for local power.

This book has identified and explored community-level conditions and circumstances that facilitate or inhibit the active engagement of residents in the public life of this city. Major findings point to the importance of opportunities for collective involvement around issues that are of ongoing and pressing concern to broad segments of the city's population as a key reason for the high levels of civic and political engagement. The following opportunities stand out as important:

1. Huge, high-profile, ongoing redevelopment projects that will fundamentally transform the city and that provide frequent and compelling occasions for public debate and action
2. Immediate threats to the ability of a longtime white ethnic working class and a new immigrant working class to live in the city, given the effects of gentrification
3. A fairly well-established—although largely unorganized—community of immigrants, mostly of color and linguistically diverse, who have been in the city for two decades or more and who intend to remain and become politically engaged there
4. A growing professional, largely white middle class that seeks both to bring new cultural, educational, and environmental amenities and attractions to the city and to retain the appeal of its racial-ethnic and class diversity
5. A relatively open space for collective action by residents, created in part by the absence of a dominant local business sector and a city government still hampered by a changing but still present system of patronage politics, plus limited resources

Overall, these findings and other evidence from this study suggest that people in urban communities are moved to active engagement in public life when important matters are at stake, discussions and decisions about those matters are highly visible, the potential for change carries both benefits and dangers that are readily recognizable by many members of the community, residents hold elements of a common vision so that shared action carries the potential for productive outcomes, and local institutions offer a space for collective action.

I devote the rest of this chapter to the larger implications of these findings—implications that connect back to the two main concepts I have used throughout this book. The first implication has to do with shared governance and how it relates to politically engaged voluntary associations choosing when to collaborate with government, when to act independently from government, and when to actually take part in governance. The second is about a stated commitment to incorporate newer immigrant groups into some aspects of community (social citizenship) life while excluding them from full membership, especially in regard to local politics.

The voluntary associations I studied involve people directly in collective political action. Consistent with what most scholars mean when they acknowledge that a subset of civil society associations are political, their actions included taking stands on political issues and mobilizing people to advocate with city government for those issues. I could not completely reconcile what I saw happening in Somerville as limited to a prevailing view that states, "Civil society has no formal power, but rather rests on the ability to exert influence on decision-makers" (Cohen and Arato 1994: 268). To this way of thinking, however much civil society associations might influence public decisions, actually making those decisions is a function left to government, to the state, alone.

Because what I saw and heard in Somerville did not seem well captured by a solely state-centered notion of politics, I searched instead for some other framework. This led me to a relatively new literature focused on the concept of governance.[10] This literature connects associational activity (civil society) and governmental (state) activity in a relationship of mutually shared power. Public decision making becomes a product of dynamic and ongoing engagement by multiple involved actors, both inside and outside government.[11] It was at this point that I began using the term shared governance as a way to make larger sense of my data.

I became especially interested in associational engagement that seemed aimed directly toward making public decisions beyond influencing the making of those decisions by the local state. For example, Chapter 3 tells the story of the coalition of community associations that organized a public forum separate from the city's "official" forum to develop their own vision for the future of this changing city. I suggested that this coalition of civil society associations sought not only to influence political decision makers but also to be included as decision makers. I described how the Mystic View

Task Force assumed a legally sanctioned position as a public decision maker in relation to the city's largest redevelopment project.

Even when shared governance does not go as far as including non-state actors as actual decision makers in regard to public issues, the concept of shared governance differs substantially from the two most commonly held notions about the role of voluntary associations in relation to politics. The first sees associations mainly as providing a site for deliberation of public issues—a deliberation that occurs before the official decisions are subsequently made by government.[12] The second sees voluntary associational activity as primarily about political socialization—that is, acquiring civic skills and virtues that prepare people for possible future involvement in politics, as defined by the state.[13] While I recognize the value of both the deliberative and the political socialization functions of associations, they are quite different from direct participation in the making of decisions captured by the concept of shared governance.

There is a growing literature on a role for voluntary associations in what is called collaborative governance.[14] As I have said, associations I studied sometimes choose to collaborate with local government and other times choose not to collaborate. In this way, they retain autonomy as civil society organizations, distinct from the state. Since the term collaborative governance excludes the option of non-collaboration, I have used the term shared governance instead. I mean this to offer associations a wider range of relationships with government, as I observed in my research. These relationships can include being adversaries as well as partners (Ostrander 2012).

The making of "hard choices on whether to work with or against the state" (Hendriks 2006: 487) allows voluntary associations to retain their autonomy while still seeking to influence government and/or to become decision makers alongside government. This cautious connection to the state allows the associations to avoid being co-opted by the state, avoids dependence on government's invitation to participate, and allows for both consensus and conflict approaches to achieving goals. Voluntary associations may be wary of collaborations with government because they do not trust government's willingness to accede real power and they are concerned about the threat of government co-optation of resident initiatives and the vulnerability of government-initiated (and thus government-controlled) ventures (Newman et al. 2004). As one scholar stated, "Unless those engaged in collaboration have the political power to defend the structures and resources that make collaboration possible, they can be scaled back and eliminated in the face of tightening budgets, unfavorable elections, or shifting fashions in public administration" (Weir 2010).

I now turn to the second of the larger implications of my findings: incorporation by local communities of newer immigrant groups into some aspects of public life while these groups are still excluded from full social citizenship. The experiences of older (Irish and Italian) versus newer (Brazilian, Latino, and Haitian) immigrants in Somerville show how participation has changed over time, both in terms of how well accepted new immigrants are compared with older immigrant groups and in terms of how issues such as race and language affect that acceptance. My interviews, observations at community meetings, and other data all show that newer immigrants are, to some extent, civically and politically active in the urban community I studied. At the same time, even those newer immigrants who have been city residents for twenty years or more and hold legal citizenship are not fully participating members of the community, that is, they lack full social citizenship. They are entirely absent from elected positions in the local body politic.

The relative exclusion of immigrants in today's Somerville is starkly shown by the limited occasions under which newer immigrant groups become most actively engaged in public life. Most telling is the finding that the most frequent occasions for immigrant engagement are periodic local events that immediately threaten immigrant safety and security, such as raids by federal Immigration and Customs Enforcement agents and the passage of local ordinances that immigrants perceive as threatening. Other research has shown that immigrants increase their political engagement when their political and economic interests are directly threatened (Pantoja, Ramirez, and Segura 2001). If such actions by immigrants resulted in more sustained engagement in public life, then these actions might count as a positive outcome—but acting largely or solely to defend one's own life and livelihood is evidence not of acceptance or inclusion, not of open opportunities and support for continued engagement, but rather of exclusion from social citizenship as well as participation in local shared governance. As others have shown, where immigrants and other political newcomers gain full and genuine access to membership and acceptance, to full social citizenship, then they are able to "act autonomously . . . for the common good, rather than out of . . . immediate material needs" (Glenn 2000: 7).

Important as the active engagement by immigrant leaders I have examined in this book is, meaningful civic engagement must include access to the political system, including access to elected positions in local government (Mark R. Warren 2001: 28). Active engagement, even to the point of taking part in actual public decision making—to what I have called shared governance—is, as I have said, not a substitute for government. It does not replace government's power, but rather shares it.[15]

For newer immigrants to be elected to political office, immigrant leaders (and non-immigrant allies who support them) must develop an explicit political mobilization strategy. As discussed earlier in this chapter, this has not yet occurred in Somerville, although future possibilities exist. Until this happens, immigrant concerns here, as elsewhere, are far less likely to be heard and addressed (American Political Science Association 2004: 11; Hardy-Fanta and Martinez 2002).

As with any group, when newer immigrants are markedly less engaged in their local communities than are other residents, a strong and full democracy is simply not possible. In contrast to those who say that immigrants should be entitled to become civically and politically engaged only when they become legal citizens, I argue instead that local communities benefit from active engagement, even by non-citizens. This means that cities with substantial populations of newer immigrants must act affirmatively to incorporate them into public life. They can do so by openly acknowledging the barriers that immigrants face and the threat to local democracy that occurs when large numbers of residents are not involved in community affairs (Bloemraad 2006) and then moving to address those barriers with changes in local policies and practices like those I have suggested several times in this book. Other scholars have argued that new thinking about governance beyond government contributes to extending opportunities for civic and political engagement to non-citizens (Garcia 2006).

At its heart, this book is about the practice of local democracy. Other scholars have argued that democracy more generally develops from active engagement by people at the local level. When people participate in the civic and political life of their own communities, they construct a strong foundation for democracy overall. A common belief is that small to medium cities, such as Somerville, hold special promise for urban democracy (King 2004). As one scholar has argued, "The starting point . . . is at the local level, not because local action is sufficient but because it provides the necessary grounding for democracy" (Mark R. Warren 2001: 22).[16] Participation most often means participation in voluntary associations, which many see as "the underpinning of a robust democracy" (Ramakrishnan and Bloemraad 2008a: 2).

Democracy at the national and even the global level depends, then, on local communities acting together to build democratic participation from the ground up.[17] The most effective way to get people to participate in public life is to engage them around local issues that affect their daily lives and their immediate local environment (Smock 2004: 226). Especially for those who have not previously been engaged, local participation is typically the starting point for participation at higher levels.[18] In the absence of their participation and the full acceptance into the community that participation requires, democracy itself weakens[19] (Andersen 2008: 77; Bloemraad 2006). In other words, a failure to extend social citizenship to all who live in a community is also a failure of democracy.[20]

Notes

CHAPTER 1: INTRODUCTION

1. Some scholars see voluntary associations as located in some "social" sphere separate from (and adverse to) government and politics and disconnected from efforts to affect public issues (Skocpol and Fiorina 1999; Theiss-Morse and Hibbing 2005: 228). Maintaining a conceptual and definitional separation between politics and civil society has the advantage of allowing the assessment of how actions in one realm affect actions in the other. Some researchers have claimed that individuals who are civically engaged are more likely to become politically engaged as well. Recent evidence, however, showed that civic engagement leads to political engagement only when that civic engagement is explicitly "political" (e.g., discussing and taking stands on political issues). Civic engagement that is not political (e.g., volunteering by helping others, belonging to a social, cultural, or other non-political association) does not seem to be strongly connected to becoming politically engaged (Sobieraj and White 2007; Walker 2008). Fung (2003a: 535) articulated this as a debate between "tame and mischievous associative democrats."

2. Irene Bloemraad argued similarly that what holds a community together is a notion of citizenship not as a legal status but as an "identity that provides a sense of belonging" and as "an invitation to participate in a system of mutual governance" (2006: 1). I use the term shared governance as a synonym for "mutual governance consistent with other literature."

3. British sociologist T. H. Marshall defined the term social citizenship as "the right to a modicum of economic security and to share in the full social heritage and to live the life of a civilized being, according to the standards prevailing in the society" (1964: 78; cited in Glenn 2000: 7). Here I use Glenn's (2000, 2011) and Bloemraad's (2006) revision of that term.

4. In Somerville, the largest Latino group is from El Salvador. Brazilians are not considered Latinos because they speak Portuguese rather than Spanish.

5. Ansell and Gash 2008; Boyte 2005; Fox and Ward 2008; Fung and Wright 2001; Garcia 2006; Sirianni 2009; Taylor 2007.

6. As political scientist Jeff Berry wrote, "In today's cities, citizen participation is really nonprofit participation" (Berry 2003: 114).

7. Europe's Organisation for Economic Co-operation and Development (OCED) defined governance as "the process by which citizens collectively solve their problems and meet society's needs, using government as an instrument" (2001: 11).

8. Cohen and Rogers 1995; Diamond 1999; Putnam 1995, 2000; Verba, Schlozman, and Brady 1995; Skocpol 2003; Wuthnow 1998, 2002.

9. Speaking at an open microphone, a resident at a community meeting that I attended in June 2009 said, "We're not Slumerville anymore. The mayor has brought us up, and we need to stay there."

10. During the period of my research, two women and nine men served on the Somerville Board of Aldermen. The elected School Committee had three women and six men. As I have said, one woman (of Irish descent) has served as Somerville's mayor.

11. These raids continued into the fall of 2010, when federal ICE agents entered an apartment building in the middle of the night in search of a tenant who had allegedly committed a crime. When questioned by the agents, terrified residents said that the person no longer lived there.

12. I consider first-generation people as those who were born outside the United States and immigrated to the United States. Second-generation individuals were born in the United States of foreign-born parents. Third-generation individuals were born in the United States of United States–born parents and foreign-born grandparents.

13. See Green 2007a.

14. At the same time, in November 2010, after extensive organizing of local immigrant youth by Somerville community organizations Centro Presente and the Welcome Project, both the Somerville School Committee and the more conservative Board of Aldermen unanimously passed a resolution supporting the federal DREAM Act. This act would provide a path to citizenship for undocumented youth brought to the United States by their parents as young children who commit to pursuing higher education or military service. One longtime alderman tried to block the affirmative vote by raising a procedural issue, but once it was clear that the resolution was going to pass, he cast his vote in favor. Also in October 2012, the Board of Aldermen unanimously passed a resolution rejecting the use of the term "illegal" to describe undocumented immigrants in Somerville (Centro Presente, press release, October 26, 2012, www.cpresente.org/news-publications/press releases, accessed October 26, 2012).

15. Ansell and Gosh 2008; Fung 2003a, 2003b; Fung and Wright 2001; Sirianni 2009.

16. Occasional notes throughout this book provide updates on key matters considered here. This information was obtained largely from publicly available sources, such as local newspapers.

CHAPTER 2: OVERVIEW OF HISTORY, DEMOGRAPHICS, AND POLITICS

1. Renowned urban sociologist Herbert Gans wrote: "Towns are sometimes differentiated from cities, but otherwise, there is no consensus about when they are small enough not to be called cities" (Gans 2009: 213). The distinction other than "town" that I used in my decision to call Somerville a "city" is the alternative characterization of it as an inner-ring suburb of Boston. While Somerville is part of the greater Boston metropolitan area, it is a separate political entity, with its own distinct history and culture and with few of the characteristics reflected in the term "suburb" (Hanlon 2009).

2. One-third of Somerville's total population of 77,000 (26,000 people) is thought to be foreign born or immigrant. Twenty percent of 26,000 is 5,200, or fewer than one-third of the city's estimated 13,235 non-citizens in 2007.

3. The years 2005 and 2007 are U.S. Census Community Survey estimates.

4. Thirty-four percent of East Somerville residents are non-white, and over 20 percent are Hispanic (OSPCD 2008: 196) compared with West Somerville (particularly the Davis Square area), whose population is nearly 90 percent white (Office of the Mayor 2008: 42). On East Somerville's main thoroughfare, called Broadway, Portuguese and Spanish are heard as often as is English, and Brazilian and other Latin American food is widely available. Early each morning, Latino immigrant men gather in East Somerville's Foss Park in the hope of being picked up for day labor.

5. The chief left Somerville in 2009 to return to Florida to accept a higher post.

CHAPTER 3: MAJOR REDEVELOPMENT, COMMUNITY INVOLVEMENT, AND SHARED GOVERNANCE

1. Civic engagement scholars define voluntary associations as freely formed, somewhat structured volunteer membership groups (Smith, Stubbins, and Dover 2006; Wuthnow 1991). Those I discuss here act for public benefit, although members may, of course, share in those public benefits. Associations differ from formally constituted nonprofit organizations (e.g., community development corporations or social service agencies) in that they are usually more informal and have a less hierarchical governing and leadership structure; in addition, associations rely largely on their volunteer members to carry out their activities, whereas community nonprofits usually rely largely on paid staff. If an association has access to paid staff through a sponsoring organization, as two of those I discuss here do, the principles of community organizing dictate that staffers take their lead from members—though this may or may not occur in practice.

2. One of the main debates about community development corporations (CDCs) is how to balance their dual roles as developers and community organizers (Melendez and Servon 2007). When, for example, they build new housing or rehabilitate older affordable housing units, CDCs depend on local government for a portion of the financing and for various permits related to zoning and other concerns. At the same time, in their organizing and advocacy role, CDCs sometimes develop an adversarial relationship with that same government. Somerville's CDC appeared to deal with this situation partly by creating satellite voluntary associations that keep their organizing separate from their role as housing developers, at least to some extent. It is those associ-

ations that are the subject here. At the SCC's 2008 annual meeting, which I attended, the executive director acknowledged the delicate balance between the organization's two sometimes contradictory roles, remarking, with characteristic humor, "Part of my job is to get into hot water. This is the fine line we walk."

3. In February 2011, the *Boston Sunday Globe* reported that the project was proceeding apace (Moskowitz 2011). As of July 2011, local newspapers reported, "Assembly Square Development is on track" (Kane 2011). In early January 2012, Somerville's mayor said, "Assembly Square will be a neighborhood for all" (Firestone 2012).

4. In July 2012, IKEA pulled out of the plan to build a Somerville store. News sources reported, "The announcement did not surprise Somerville officials," and FRIT said they would consider buying the property (Ross 2012).

5. In 2002, HUD designated Union Square a Neighborhood Revitalization Strategy Area. This enabled the city to obtain Community Development Block Grant (CDBG) monies toward proceeding with redevelopment.

6. At a meeting of the AHOC I attended in May 2009, the small group (six people plus the Somerville Community Corps organizer) celebrated the increase in planned affordable housing for Union Square as a "victory for AHOC." At the same time, attendees were "disappointed that," as one put it, "we had not pushed for a commitment to a displacement policy" before the city decided about Union Square rezoning. Everyone present acknowledged that they had not sustained their energy and had gotten tired "toward the end."

7. The struggle between Somerville and the state of Massachusetts over the Green Line continued as of August 2011, when the Massachusetts Bay Transportation Authority announced another delay of the Green Line extension, now slated to begin in fall 2018 at the earliest (Byrne 2011). The mayor of Somerville reiterated the state's legal obligation to complete the project, called on the governor to intervene, and urged Somerville residents to make their feelings known to state officials. Legally, the state is still bound by the earlier lawsuit to a 2014 completion (Byrne 2011). In his 2012 inaugural address, the mayor of Somerville said, "The Green Line will get done, but we will have to fight for it, advocate for it and push for it—every single day" (Joseph A. Curtatone, Mayor of Somerville. 2012 Inaugural Address. Available at www.somervillema.gov/departments/mayor/speeches).

8. See Cohen and Arato 1994; Diamond 1999; Putnam 1995; Skocpol and Fiorina 1999; Stolle and Rochon 1998.

9. For example, meetings of ESNC that I attended in 2008 and 2009 were less diverse, even though they were held in the area where most immigrants lived. Meetings usually attracted about ten people, nearly all white Anglos, except for the Haitian woman who chaired the group. She was eager to recruit more attendees and set about planning an event aimed at doing so at the local Salvadoran church.

CHAPTER 4: OLD AND NEW IMMIGRANT EXPERIENCES, TODAY AND YESTERDAY

1. The museum exhibit was mounted in the winter of 2007. It consisted of oral histories of old and new immigrants, photos, and other artifacts. Under my guidance and that of Deborah Pacini Hernandez, professor of anthropology at Tufts University,

students conducted fourteen of the forty-five interviews referenced in this book originally for the Immigrant City, Then and Now, exhibit. In 2008, I was asked to join the board of directors of the Welcome Project, where (as of 2012) I continue to serve.

2. Recall from Chapter 1 that I consider first-generation people as those who were born outside the United States and immigrated to the United States. Second-generation individuals were born in the United States of foreign-born parents. Third-generation individuals were born in the United States of United States–born parents and foreign-born grandparents.

3. I am grateful to sociologist Anna Sandoval Giron for calling my attention to this concept and its possible benefit to my study.

4. This chapter is about first-generation Latino, Brazilian, and Haitian immigrant residents today compared with second- and third-generation Irish and Italian descendants of immigrant parents or grandparents. I recognize that nationality, race, ethnicity, and class interact in complex ways, even though I do not explore each distinction and entanglement at every point in the stories of these different groups. Virtually everyone I talked to understood that immigrants of color encounter barriers that white immigrants do not. Because a working-class background is valued in Somerville as part of the city's heritage, as well as its immigrant heritage, class is an especially complicated (and fascinating) category with respect to the different immigrant groups. Most of the second- and third-generation descendants of Irish and Italian ancestors in this study are middle class, even though they may still identify as working class, and all are white. First-generation Latino, Brazilian, and Haitian immigrants see themselves and are seen by others as "people of color," and most identify as working class.

5. I am not suggesting that it is especially unusual for people to subjectively identify with classes to which they do not objectively belong. Sociologists know that "social classes are subjective reconstructions of objective circumstances. . . . Two people with the same objective levels of income, education, and occupation may perceive themselves to be members of different social classes" (Walsh, Jennings, and Stoker 2004: 470; Wright 1997). My use of the concept of "imaginary" allows me to uncover how claiming a working-class identity while benefiting from middle-class privileges provides political advantage in a context (such as Somerville) where a working-class heritage is valued, even idealized.

6. The word "guinea" had long referred to African slaves, but by the late 1890s, the term was increasingly used in a pejorative way for southern Europeans, especially southern Italians (Barrett and Roediger 1997: 7).

CHAPTER 5: IMMIGRANT CIVIC AND POLITICAL ENGAGEMENT

1. A local Somerville observer reflected this idea when he explained why immigrants who are eligible to vote may not do so: "Most who are eligible to vote are so preoccupied with the daily challenges of economic survival and family maintenance that they have little attention for politics" (quoted in Shelton 2007).

2. Voting by non-citizens was widespread in the United States for the first 150 years of our history. The U.S. Constitution gives states and municipalities the right to decide who is eligible to vote (Hayduk and Wucker 2004). From 1776 to 1926, twenty-two states and territories allowed non-citizens to vote in local, state, and even federal

elections. This right was gradually repealed as a result of anti-immigrant sentiment during the late nineteenth and early twentieth centuries and replaced with the idea that immigrants should prove their loyalty before being allowed to vote. Today, twenty countries around the world allow non-citizen voting, including the entire European Union. In Massachusetts, Cambridge, Newton, and Amherst passed resolutions allowing non-citizen voting, but they were blocked by the state legislature.

3. Canada may also be more welcoming to immigrants because of its need to increase its population (Bloemraad 2006: 122).

4. The proposed federal DREAM Act aims to address the barrier to higher education for the children of undocumented immigrants. It would allow children brought to the United States under the age of sixteen by their undocumented parents a path to U.S. citizenship if they live here at least five years, finish high school, show good moral character, become enrolled in an institution of higher learning, or enter military service. It is supported by numerous college presidents and the U.S. military. The act passed the U.S. House of Representatives in December 2010. It received a fifty-five to forty-one majority vote in the U.S. Senate, but failed to become law when it fell short of the sixty votes needed to prevent an opposing filibuster. President Obama is working to revive the act (Preston 2011). It is estimated that the act would affect 800,000 of the total estimated 11 million unauthorized young immigrants currently residing in the United States (Sacchetti 2010a) [see http://dreamact.info/students]. Connecticut is the latest state to open up opportunities for the children of undocumented immigrants to attend public higher-education institutions at the in-state rate (Cheney 2011). A similar bill has been proposed in Massachusetts. Critics argue that this would amount to a giveaway to students who are in the United States illegally, while legal out-of-state residents would be paying a higher rate of tuition by comparison. They also argue that measures such as these encourage more "illegal aliens" to come to the United States to take advantage of such opportunities.

5. An estimated 4.5 million illegal immigrants nationwide are driving regularly, mostly without licenses, according to an analysis by the *New York Times*. Only three states currently issue driver's licenses without asking for proof of legal residency in the United States: New Mexico, Utah, and Washington. As a result, at least 30,000 undocumented residents who were stopped for common traffic violations in the three years between 2008 and 2010 ended up being deported, according to the Department of Homeland Security (Preston and Gebeloff 2010).

6. However, in October 2010, after I had left the research field, not only the School Committee but also the Somerville Board of Aldermen passed a resolution in support of the federal DREAM Act described earlier. They did so unanimously, after a youth organizing campaign led by Centro Presente and the Welcome Project that ran for a number of months. I attended the Board of Aldermen meeting where two undocumented students currently attending Somerville High School spoke compellingly about the limits they faced, especially in relation to their desire to acquire a college education, as a result of their illegal status.

7. The 1975 U.S. Voting Rights Act guarantees access to ballots, instructions, and voter information in one's own language *if* in the political jurisdiction at least 10,000 people or 5 percent of the population speak a language other than English. The Voting Rights Act applies only to American Indians, Asians, Alaskan natives, and

people of Spanish heritage. It excludes the largest non–English speaking population in Somerville and in Massachusetts—Portuguese-speaking Brazilians (Bloemraad 2006: 134–135)—and it does not explicitly include people who speak Haitian Creole. Cities in Massachusetts that are required to provide Spanish-speaking voters access include Lawrence, Holyoke, Springfield, and Boston, but not Somerville (Ao 2007).

8. The police chief hired in 2008 left Somerville to return to Florida in December 2009. The new police chief's position on Secure Communities was not yet clear.

9. Fear can extend to local police, even when they have pledged (as in Somerville) not to actively enforce federal immigration law. One day I was attending a meeting with a group of Somerville immigrant advocates held at a local coffee shop. A very tall, white police officer in uniform came into the shop, asking loudly, "Who owns that car?" as he pointed to a vehicle parked across the street. A small Latina woman in our group stood up, obviously shaking, and said, in a frightened voice, "I do." The officer said, "Come with me." After she left with the officer, one of the immigrant advocates asked the rest of us, "She's a citizen, right?" No one spoke. He said, "I think I better go out there. [The police] know who I am." As it turned out, the woman's car had been bumped by another vehicle, and the police officer was trying to be helpful by letting her know. But, the fear that the incident provoked was nevertheless an example of the fear that brown-skinned immigrants live with every day.

10. A lawsuit against the company where these workers were employed resulted in their receipt of $850,000 in back wages. Of the 361 workers detained, 168 were deported, twenty-six have deportation orders, and sixteen had their immigration status adjusted to allow them to remain in the United States (Ballon 2008).

11. Somerville's Human Rights Commission set up the Immigrant Dialogue Group. As it was described to me, most attendees are immigrant service providers from various community nonprofit organizations.

12. Since I completed my research at the end of 2009, Centro Presente, which moved to the city quite recently, has moved in this direction, in collaboration with other Somerville organizations.

13. In November 2010, after I left the research field, several immigrant organizations came together to urge and then sponsor the mayor's framing and formal signing of a proclamation acknowledging the importance of immigrant contributions to Somerville. Announced at an event held at City Hall on a Saturday afternoon as "A Rally with Mayor Curtatone," the event was well attended by a diverse audience representing constituencies of Centro Presente, the Welcome Project, the Haitian Coalition, Somerville Community Corps, and Community Action Agency of Somerville. These are the organizations with the credibility, although perhaps not the current capacity, to politically mobilize the city's diverse immigrant groups.

CHAPTER 6: GENTRIFICATION, RESIDENT DISPLACEMENT, AND A COMMON VISION FOR THE CITY'S FUTURE

1. As I note in Chapter 1, these three categories that people call "the three Somervilles" are, of course, complex. For example, not all of the city's old-time Irish and Italians are averse to the changes that gentrification brings or insensitive to barriers faced by immigrants of color. A few of the newer Latino, Brazilian, and Haitian immigrants

have moved into the middle class. A number of the people who older residents call yuppies (young urban professionals) are actually middle aged. While residents from the city's growing professional middle class are often progressives who, for example, advocate policies that would facilitate the election of newer immigrant candidates to political office and support more affordable housing, some members of the new middle class would oppose these efforts. I use these three categories, then, as many Somervillians do, as ideal types.

2. In neighboring affluent Cambridge, for example, one-third of the city budget is from property taxes on residences. Most of the rest derives from property taxes on commercial buildings.

3. The April 2009 city report *Trends in Somerville* estimates population growth of 3 percent, or 2,398 new residents, between the 2000 and 2030 (OSPCD 2009b: 13).

4. "Affordable" is defined by the state of Massachusetts as costing a family one-third of the city's median income. In 2000, the median income for a family of four was $52,500 (Powers and Danseyar 2001).

5. When, in July 1999, Starbucks proposed to move into Davis Square, which it did soon after, "some Davis Square Task Force members said they would support a Starbucks as long as it was a good neighbor, [and] others were open about their distaste for the chain which has been seen as a harbinger of gentrification." Residents also expressed concern about the possible effect of Starbucks on two independent coffee shops already in Davis Square (Wamunyu 1999).

CHAPTER 7: EXTENDING SOCIAL CITIZENSHIP, REMAKING CITY GOVERNANCE

1. It has sometimes been argued that newer immigrants are less civically and politically engaged because of their political experiences in their country of origin before they came to the United States. While this factor cannot be completely ruled out, immigrant leaders I spoke with rarely mentioned it, and some current research concludes, to quote one example, "The results provide no evidence that political experience prior to migration inhibits engagement in the new host country, regardless of country of origin and regardless of how long immigrants lived there before migrating" (White et al. 2008: 278).

2. While this book has focused on the absence of Somerville's newer immigrants in the city's civic and political life, evidence such as this calls attention to their economic exclusion as well, in terms of lack of access to city jobs.

3. Statements about Somerville politics often contain thinly veiled references to the city's past, when government was indeed corrupt and the role of the Winter Hill Gang was evident. For example, when U.S. Congressman Mike Capuano, a former Somerville mayor, ran (unsuccessfully) for the U.S. Senate after the death of Senator Edward Kennedy, the *Boston Globe* described Capuano (a Dartmouth College graduate) as "more Somerville than Dartmouth," perhaps because of his history of "running for office in Somerville, a city where politics is . . . often a contact sport" (Rezendes 2009).

4. An active city resident I talked with had gone door-to-door one year to register people to vote in East Somerville, an area with many immigrants. She estimated

that, of the area's approximately 10,000 residents, an unknown number of whom are legal citizens who are eligible to register and vote, only about one-third (3,500) were registered.

5. Some research shows that it takes two decades from the time a minority population becomes a majority to elect a minority candidate (Logan and Mollenkopf 2003). Actions at the local level are known to be important to immigrant political engagement, especially "the degree of access to local government and the degree to which city government and political actions reach out to immigrant communities" (Ramakrishnan and Bloemraad 2008b: 64).

6. This view of the conflict within Somerville's Democratic Party was also the conclusion of a political analyst writing for the *Boston Globe*: "As in lots of Somerville elections, it's often less about principles and policies than the principals and their political allies" (Jonas 2008).

7. This means, apparently, white Anglo "blue collar," because most newer immigrants are, of course, "blue collar" working class.

8. In November 2004, the same year the new mayor was elected, the PDS succeeded in electing their young candidate for state representative over a longtime incumbent. In 2005, they were able to gain one-third of the city's Democratic Convention delegate seats (Parker 2005a). The then-leader of the PDS was quoted as saying that they did not want to take over Somerville's Democratic Party: "We just want to work with everybody" (Parker 2005a). Another key win came in November 2005, when a PDS candidate for ward alderman defeated a twenty-two-year incumbent (Healy 2005). The defeated incumbent later successfully ran for alderman-at-large in the campaign that was described as having turned ugly against a young Latino candidate who also happened to be a co-founder of the PDS. Ironically, the alderman-at-large seat opened because the person who had held it, another PDS candidate, had also been elected to the state legislature.

9. How organizations become more diverse is a valuable topic for future research. Some research also shows how nonprofit groups focused on immigrants can combine social service delivery with political advocacy and activism (De Graauw 2008).

10. Ansell and Gosh (2008); Boyte (2005); Elstub (2008); Fox and Ward (2008); Fung and Wright (2001); Garcia (2006); Sirianni (2009); Taylor (2007).

11. Foucault's concept of governmentality is relevant here. In this view, civic actors are seen in relation to multiple sites of governing, beyond the traditional boundaries of the state (or in this case, local) government (McKee 2009: 469). This newer thinking is also consistent with notions of democracy that go beyond the state, toward a democratic society (Boyte 2005).

12. See Cohen and Arato (1994); Diamond (1999); Putnam (1995); and Stolle and Rochen (1998).

13. See, for example, Burns, Schlozman, and Verba (2001) and Verba, Schlozman, and Brady (1995).

14. Ansell and Gash (2008); Fung and Wright (2001); Sirianni (2009).

15. The concept of shared governance "reframes the debate between participatory and representative democracy by highlighting the importance of both" (Boyte 2005: 541).

16. There are limitations, of course, to local politics: "Critics of localism argue

that national organizing is necessary to adequately address the social and economic forces shaping localities" (Mark R. Warren 2009: 119). And "in an increasingly globalized world . . . not all problems can be addressed at the community level" (Smock 2004: 222). For a useful discussion of when and how to connect local organizing to broader movements for social change, see Smock 2004: chapter 8.

17. Elstub (2008: 181); King (2004); Mark R. Warren (2001: 21).

18. Hardy-Fanta (2002: 196); Portney and Berry (1997); Mark R. Warren (2001: 22).

19. "[The] political system's stability and democratic values are threatened if high rates of immigration produce large numbers of nonparticipating, unrepresented, disengaged residents" (Andersen 2008: 77).

20. Some scholars refer to urban or local citizenship (Garcia 2006). I do not mean to suggest that simply "adding" immigrant participation to current political systems is sufficient for democratic reform, although it is, in my view, necessary. I agree with those who argue that, as one scholar has stated, "in reducing barriers and gaining access to politics, we cannot neglect to reconstruct the politics we seek to influence" (Junn 1999: 1434). Except for the rather modest, although not yet implemented, measures suggested here—such as routine language translation and the option of noncitizen voting in local elections—that political reconstruction is beyond the scope of this book.

References

Abel, David. 2009. "Budget Misery Grows for Cities and Towns." *Boston Globe*, October 17.

Ackerman, Meghan. 2007. "Will You Afford to Live Here?" *Somerville Journal*, July 26.

Agarwal, Nisha. 2004. "Somerville, Massachusetts: The Next Front on the Zoning Battle." *Segregation and Integration* 9 (November): Available at http://www.americancity.org/print_version.php. Accessed June 27, 2007.

Aizenman, N. C. 2007. "U.S Immigrant Raids Spur Fears in Children." *Boston Globe*, April 3.

———. 2009. "Number of Children Born to Illegal Immigrants Jumps." *Boston Globe*, April 15.

American Political Science Association. 2004. Task Force on Inequality and American Democracy. *American Democracy in an Age of Rising Inequality.* Available at http://www.apsanet.org.

Andersen, Kristi. 2008. "Parties, Organizations, and the Political Incorporation of Immigrants in Six Cities," in *Civic Hopes and Political Realities: Immigrants, Community Organizations, and Political Engagement,* edited by S. Karthick Ramakrishnan and Irene Bloemraad, 77–106. New York: Russell Sage Foundation.

Ansell, Chris, and Alison Gosh. 2008. "Collaborative Governance in Theory and Practice." *Journal of Public Administration and Theory* 18, no. 4 (October): 543–572.

Ao, Terry M. 2007. "When the Voting Rights Act Became Un-American: The Misguided Vilification of Section 203, Views on the 2006 Reauthorization of the Voting Rights Act." *Alabama Law Review* 58 (2): 377–379.

Ballon, Brian R. 2008. "Raided Factory, Workers Make Deal on Owed OT." *Boston Globe*, November 19.

Barreto, Matt A. 2003. "Re-examining the 'Politics of In-between': Political Participation among Mexican Immigrants in the United States." *Journal of Behavioral Sciences* 25, no. 4 (November): 427–447.

Barrett, James R., and David Roediger. 1997. "In-between Peoples: Race, Nationality and the 'New Immigrant' Working Class." *Journal of American Ethnic History* 16 (Spring): 3–44.

Bennett, Philip. 1993. "Tugging at the Welcome Mat: Some in Somerville Say 'Sanctuary' Time Is Over." *Boston Globe*, September 28.

Berg, Bruce L. 2009. *Qualitative Research Methods for Social Science.* Boston: Allyn and Bacon.

Berry, Jeffrey M. 2003. *A Voice for Nonprofits.* Washington, DC: Brookings Institute.

Betancur, John L. 2002. "The Politics of Gentrification: The Case of West Town in Chicago." *Urban Affairs Review* 37, no. 6 (July): 780–814.

Bierman, Noah, and Maria Sacchetti. 2010. "Senate Vote Hits Illegal Residents." *Boston Globe*, May 28.

Bloemraad, Irene. 2006. *Becoming a Citizen: Incorporating Immigrants and Refugees in the U.S. and Canada.* Berkeley: University of California Press.

Boyte, Harry C. 2005. "Reframing Democracy: Governance, Civic Agency, and Politics." *Public Administration Review* 65 (5): 536–546.

Burns, Nancy, Kay Lehman Schlozman, and Sidney Verba. 2001. *The Private Roots of Public Action: Gender, Equality, and Political Participation.* Cambridge, MA: Harvard University Press.

Byrne, Matt. 2011. "Green Line Extension Put off until 2018." *Boston Globe*, August 2.

Cameron, Stuart, and Jon Coaffee. 2005. "Art, Gentrification and Regeneration—From Artist as Pioneer to Public Arts." *European Journal of Housing Policy* 5, no. 1 (April): 39–58.

Carroll, Matt. 2007. "Your Town: Percentage of Students Whose First Language Is Not English." *Boston Globe*, December 23.

Chabot, Hillary. 2002a. "Depot Developers Threaten Walk." *Somerville Journal*, October 3.

———. 2002b. "21 Inches." *Somerville Journal*, December 5.

———. 2003. "Phantom Gang Unit Gets Staff." *Somerville Journal*, April 10.

———. 2010. "Critics Blast Governor on Illegals." *Boston Herald*, July 21.

Chaskin, Robert J. 2003. "Fostering Neighborhood Democracy: Legitimacy and Accountability within Loosely Coupled Systems." *Nonprofit and Voluntary Sector Quarterly* 32, no. 2 (June): 161–189.

Cheney, Kyle. 2011. "Mass. Immigrant Advocates Applaud Conn. Tuition Law." *Boston Globe*, June 17.

Choup, Anne Marie. 2006. "Calculated Risks: Why Civic Leaders (Re)Turn to Politics." *International Political Science Review* 27, no. 3 (July): 285–300.

City of Somerville. 2005a. Press release, March 7, 2005. Available at www.somervillema.gov/news. Accessed August 28, 2008.

———. 2005b. Press release, May 18, 2005. Available at www.somervillema.gov/news. Accessed August 28, 2008.

———. 2010. Press release, March 1, 2010. "Community Process Generates Somerville's First Vision Statement." Available at www.somervillema.gov/Section.cfm?org=OSPCD&page=1510.

Cohen, Jean L., and Andrew Arato. 1994. *Civil Society and Political Theory.* Cambridge, MA: MIT Press.

Cohen, Joshua, and Joel Rogers. 1995. *Associations and Democracy.* London: Verso.

Commonwealth of Massachuesetts. 2004. Available at www.malegislature.gov/Laws/SessionLaws/Acts/2004/Chapter327.

Comments. 2008. "Newstalk for August 20." *The Somerville News Blog.* Available at http://somervillenews.typepad.com/the_somerville_news/2008/08/newstalk-for--2.html. Accessed August 30, 2008.

Community Corridor Planning. 2009. "Core Community Principles for Neighborhood Development Along the Green Line Corridor." Available at http://www.somervillecdc.org/WhatWeDo/CCP Principles English in Color.pdf.

"Confusion over Secure Communities." Editorial. 2010. *New York Times,* October 5.

Cooper, Marc. 2007. "Lockdown in Greeley: How Immigration Raids Terrorized a Colorado Town." *The Nation,* February 26, pp. 11–15.

Cordero-Guzman, Hector, Nina Martin, and Victoria Quiroz-Becerra. 2008. "Voting with Their Feet: Nonprofit Organizations and Immigrant Mobilization." *American Behavioral Scientist* 52, no. 4 (December): 598–617.

Crowley, Kevin T. 2009. "All-American City: How Women, Joe Six-Pack, Teachers, Clergy, and an Editor Changed Somerville Government." *Somerville Journal,* June 14.

Curtatone, Joseph A. 2004. "2004 Inaugural Address." In Mayor Curtatone's Speeches. Available at www.somervillema.gov/departments/mayor/speeches.

———. 2008. "Somerville and the Green Line: Doing Our Homework and Standing Our Ground." *Somerville News,* September 24.

DeGaetano, Alan, and Elizabeth Strom. 2003. "Comparative Urban Governance: An Integrated Approach." *Urban Affairs Review* 38, no. 3 (January): 356–395.

De Graauw, Els. 2008. "Nonprofit Organizations: Agents of Immigrant Political Incorporation in Urban America." In *Civic Hopes and Political Realities: Immigrants, Community Organizations, and Political Engagement,* edited by S. Karthick Ramakrishnan and Irene Bloemraad, 325–350. New York: Russell Sage Foundation.

de Leon, E., M. Maronick, C. J. De Vita, and E. T. Boris. 2009. *Community-Based Organizations and Immigrant Integration in the Washington, D.C., Metropolitan Area.* Washington, DC: Urban Institute.

Denzin, Norman K., and Yvonna S. Lincoln, editors. 2000. *Handbook of Qualitative Research,* 2nd ed. Thousand Oaks, CA: Sage.

Diamond, I. 1999. *Developing Democracy toward Consolidation.* Baltimore, MD: Johns Hopkins Press.

Diesenhouse, Susan. 2005. "'Slumerville' No More." *Boston Globe,* April 6.

Dreilinger, Danielle. 2007. "Drawing Immigrants out of the Shadows." *Boston Sunday Globe,* November 11.

———. 2008a. "Immigrant Workers at Risk." *Boston Sunday Globe,* October 12.

———. 2008b. "In Raid's Wake, Vow of Commitment." *Boston Sunday Globe,* August 24.

———. 2008c. "Some Fear 'Vision' of Union Square." *Boston Sunday Globe,* July 6.

Editorial. 2007. *Somerville News,* June 2.

Eisner, Deborah. 2001. "1991 Race Riot Haunts City." *Somerville Journal,* July 1.

Elstub, Stephen. 2008. "Weber's Dilemma and a Dualist Model of Deliberative and Associational Democracy." *Contemporary Political Theory* 7:169–199.

Espiritu, Yen Le. 2009. "'They're Coming to America': Immigration, Settlement, and Citizenship." *Qualitative Sociology* 32:221–227.

Esterberg, Kristin G. 2002. *Qualitative Methods in Social Research*. Boston: McGraw-Hill.

Fairclough, Julia. 2008. "Somerville's Artist Population Ranks above the National Average." *Somerville News*, January 14.

———. 2009. "From Revolution to Achievement, Somerville Is the All America City." *Somerville News*, July 1.

Farris, Ann. 2003. *A Report on Immigrant Civic Integration*. New York: Carnegie Corporation.

Federico, Meghan. 2009a. "Lowell Stop Area Residents Express Optimism, Tinged with Concern," *Somerville News*, July 23.

———. 2009b. "Somerville Prepares for the All-America City Competition." *Somerville News*, April 22.

Firestone, Andrew. 2012. "Mayor: Assembly Square Will Be a Neighborhood for All." *Somerville News*, January 11.

Flanagan, Constance, Peter Levine, and Richard Settersten. 2008. *Civic Engagement and the Changing Transition to Adulthood*. Medford, MA: CIRCLE (Center for Information and Research on Civic Learning and Engagement).

Florida, Richard. 2005. *Cities and the Creative Class*. New York: Routledge.

Foley, Michael W., and Bob Edwards. 1997. "Escape from Politics? Social Theory and the Social Capital Debate." *American Behavioral Scientist* 40 (March/April): 550–561.

Fox, Nick J., and Katie J. Ward. 2008. "What Governs Governance, and How Does It Evolve? The Sociology of Governance-in-Action." *British Journal of Sociology* 29 (3): 519–538.

Freeman, Lance. 2006. *There Goes the 'Hood: View of Gentrification from the Ground Up*. Philadelphia: Temple University Press.

Frisch, Michael, and Lisa J. Servon. 2006. "CDCs and the Changing Context for Urban Community Development: A Review of the Field and the Environment." *Community Development* 37, no. 4 (Winter): 88–107.

Fung, Archon. 2003a. "Associations and Democracy: Between Theories, Hopes, and Realities." *Annual Review of Sociology* 29:515–539.

———. 2003b. "Recipes for Public Spheres: Eight Institutional Design Choices and Their Consequences." *Journal of Political Philosophy* 11 (3): 338–367.

Fung, Archon, and Erik Olin Wright. 2001. "Deepening Democracy: Innovations in Empowered Participatory Governance." *Politics and Society* 29 (3): 5–41.

Gans, Herbert. 2009. "Some Problems of and Futures for Urban Sociology: Toward a Sociology of Settlements." *City and Community* 8 (3): 211–219.

Garcia, Marisol. 2006. "Citizenship Practices and Urban Governance in European Cities." *Urban Studies* 43, no. 4 (April): 745–765.

Gedan, Benjamin. 2004. "Law Targets Gangs in Somerville." *Boston Globe*, August 27.

———. 2005. "Somerville Mayor Reaches out to Minorities, but Is He Listening?" *Boston Globe*, February 27.

Gehrman, Elizabeth. 2009. "Top Spots to Live." *Boston Globe Magazine*, March 22, pp. 14–20.

Glenn, Evelyn Nakano. 2000. "Citizenship and Inequality: Historical and Global Perspectives." *Social Problems* 47 (1): 1–20.

———. 2011. "Constructing Citizenship: Exclusion, Subordination, and Resistance." *American Sociological Review* 76, no. 1 (February): 1–24.

Goodnough, Abby. 2010. "Immigration Crackdown Advances in a Surprising State." *New York Times*, June 11.

Gottdiener, Mark, and Ray Hutchison. 2006. *The New Urban Sociology.* Boulder, CO: Westview Press.

Green, Kristen. 2006. "City Reaches out, with Mixed Results." *Boston Globe*, May 28.

———. 2007a. "Reaching out to Rein Them In: Mayor Appeals to Younger Set to Stay in the City." *Boston Globe*, October 21.

———. 2007b. "Union Square Neighbors in the News: Neighbors Don't Want to Be Left in the Shadows." *Boston Globe*, April 29.

———. 2008. "Community Snapshot: Somerville." *Boston Sunday Globe*, July 27.

Gregory, Andrea. 2005. "Somebody Hates Yuppies." *Somerville News*, October 15.

Griffith, Jeanne M. 1995. "Gentrification: Perspectives on the Return to the Central City." *Journal of Planning Literature* 10, no. 1 (August): 241–255.

Guha, Auditi. 2009a. "Developers Told to Hold off in Somerville While a Vision for the City Is Developed." *Somerville Journal*, April 8.

———. 2009b. "PDS: One Good Outcome of the 2009 Budget Crisis." *Somerville Journal*, June 11.

———. 2009c. "State Scrambles to Meet Green Line Commitments." *Cambridge Chronicle*, August 13.

Hackworth, Jason. 2002. "Post-Recession Gentrification in New York City." *Urban Affairs Review* 37, no. 6 (July): 815–843.

Hanlon, Bernadette. 2009. "Typology of Inner-Ring Suburbs: Class, Race, and Ethnicity in U.S. Suburbia." *City and Community* 8 (3): 221–246.

Hannigan, J. 1995. "Gentrification." *Current Sociology* 43 (1): 173–182.

Hardy-Fanta, Carol. 2002. "Latina Women and Political Leadership: Implications for Latino Community Involvement." In *Latino Politics in Massachusetts: Struggles, Strategies, and Prospects*, edited by C. Hardy-Fanta and J. N. Gerson, 193–212. New York: Routledge.

Hardy-Fanta, Carol, and Jeffrey N. Gerson, editors. 2002. *Latino Politics in Massachusetts: Struggles, Strategies, and Prospects.* New York: Routledge.

Hardy-Fanta, Carol, and Robert B. Martinez. 2002. "Strategic Planning in the Community and the Courts, Holyoke." In *Latino Politics in Massachusetts: Struggles, Strategies, and Prospects*, edited by C. Hardy-Fanta and J. N. Gerson, 99–125. New York: Routledge.

Harmon, Lawrence. 2010. "Public Housing Common Sense." *Boston Globe*, September 26.

Haskell, Albert L. n.d. *Historical Guide Book of Somerville, Massachusetts.* Available at http://www.ci.somerville.ma.us/CoS_Content/documents/HaskellsHistoricalGuideBook.pdf.

Hassett, George P. 2007a. "East Somerville Organizes for the Future." *Somerville News*, June 20.

———. 2007b. "Feds Raid Local Shop; Arrest One." *Somerville News*, August 28.

———. 2007c. "More Loss in 2007." *Somerville News*, December 30.

———. 2007d. "Rapid Response Network for Illegal Immigrants Proposed." *Somerville News*, October 30.

———. 2008a. "Condo Ordinance Could Come Back." *Somerville News*, May 15.

———. 2008b. "From Gangsters to God: Pentecostal Church Will Replace Notorious Gang's Headquarters." *Somerville News*, October 1.

———. 2008c. "Residents Air Concerns on Union Square Development." *Somerville News*, December 10.

———. 2008d. "Taxes Go Up. Home Values Go Down." *Somerville News*, December 10.

Hayduck, Ron, and Michele Wucker. 2004. "Immigrant Voting Rights Receive More Attention." *Migration Information Source*, November 1. Available at http://www.migrationinformation.org/USfocus/print.cfm?ID=265.

Healy, Patrick Gerard. 2005. "For Challenger, Change Is the Ticket." *Boston Globe*, November 20.

Hendriks, Carolyn M. 2006. "Integrated Deliberation: Reconciling Civil Society's Dual Role in Deliberation." *Political Studies* 54 (3): 486–508.

Hsu, Spenser S. 2009. "Proposed Immigration Raids Delayed." *Boston Globe*, March 30.

———. 2010. "Despite Dim Prospects, Advocates Push for Immigration Bill." *Boston Globe*, February 7.

Hung, Chi-Kan Richard. 2007. "Immigrant Nonprofit Organizations in U.S. Metropolitan Areas." *Nonprofit and Voluntary Sector Quarterly* 36 (December): 707–729.

Hurst, Charles E. 2009. *Social Inequality*. New York: Allyn and Bacon.

Immergluck, Dan. 2005. "Building Power, Losing Power: The Rise and Fall of a Prominent Community Economic Development Coalition." *Economic Development Quarterly* 19, no. 3 (August): 211–224.

"It Gets Even Worse: New Anti-immigrant Laws Are Cruel, Racist, and Counterproductive." Editorial. 2011. *New York Times*, July 4.

Johnston, Carla Brooks. 2009. *Somerville, Massachusetts: Making Democracy Work.* Self-published.

Jonas, Michael, 2008. "It's the Principals, not the Principles." *Boston Globe*, May 18.

Junn, Jane. 1999. "Participation in Liberal Democracy: The Political Assimilation of Immigrants and Ethnic Minorities in the United States." *American Behavioral Scientist* 42, no. 9 (June/July):1417–1438.

Junn, Jane, and Kerry L. Haynie, editors. 2008. *New Race Politics in America: Understanding Minority and Immigrant Politics.* New York: Cambridge University Press.

Kaiser, Stephan H. 2004. *History of Transit Policies and Commitments Relative to the Central Artery Project, 1989–1992.* Available at http://www.somervillestep.org/files/HistoryCommitments1989-92_1204.pdf.

Kane, Harry. 2001. "Summer Street Controversy, Crime Statistics Highlight Ward 6 Meeting." *Somerville News*, July 6.

Kilburn, H. Whitt. 2004. "Explaining U.S. Urban Regimes: A Qualitative Comparative Analysis." *Urban Affairs Review* 39, no. 5 (May): 633–651.

King, Loren A. 2004. "Democracy and City Life," *Politics, Philosophy, and Economics* 3 (1): 97–124.

Knight, Rebecca. 2006. "Where Everybody Knows Your Name." *Financial Times*, October 13.

Knotts, H. Gibbs, and Mose Haspel. 2006. "The Impact of Gentrification on Voter Turnout." *Social Science Quarterly* 87, no. 1 (March): 110–121.

Lees, Loretta. 2008. "Gentrification and Social Mixing: Towards an Inclusive Urban Renaissance." *Urban Studies* 45, no. 12 (November): 2449–2470.

LeRoux, Kelly. 2007. "Nonprofits as Civic Intermediaries: The Role of Community-Based Organizations in Promoting Political Participation." *Urban Affairs Review* 42, no. 3 (January): 410–422.

———. 2009. "The Effects of Descriptive Representation on Nonprofits' Civic Intermediary Roles." *Nonprofit and Voluntary Sector Quarterly* 38, no. 5 (October): 741–760.

Levenstein, Charles. 1976. "Class, Suburbanization, and Ethnic Homogenization: Toward a Theory of Social-Spatial Stratification." Ph.D. dissertation, MIT, Cambridge, MA.

Levine, Peter. 2007. *The Future of Democracy: Developing the Next Generation of American Citizens.* Hanover, NH/Medford, MA: New England Press/Tufts University Press.

Light, Ivan. 2006. *Deflecting Immigration: Networks, Markets, and Regulation in Los Angeles.* New York: Russell Sage Foundation.

Lofland, John, and Lyn Lofland. 1995. *Analyzing Social Settings,* 3rd ed. Belmont, CA: Wadsworth.

Logan. J., and J. Mollenkopf. 2003. *People and Politics in America's Big Cities.* New York: Drum Major Institute.

Maislin, Josh, 2009. "Gilman Square Community Meeting Sparks Interest, Concerns." *Somerville News,* August 12.

Markusen, A., and A. Glasmeier. 2008. "Overhauling and Revitalizing Federal Economic Development Programs." *Economic Development Quarterly* 22:83–91.

Marschall, Melissa J. 2001. "Does the Shoe Fit? Testing Models of Participation for African American and Latino Involvement in Politics." *Urban Affairs Review* 37, no. 2 (November): 227–248.

Marshall, T. H. 1964. *Class, Citizenship, and Social Development.* Garden City, NY: Doubleday.

Massachusetts Immigrant and Refugee Advocacy Coalition. 2005. "Who Is at Risk of Deportation and When?" Available at http://www.miracoalition.org/issues/federal/detentiondeportation/who. Accessed January 8, 2009.

McKee, Kim. 2009. "Post-Foucaldian Governmentality: What Does It Offer Critical Social Policy Analysis?" *Critical Social Policy* 29, no. 3 (August): 465–486.

Melendez, Edwin, and Lisa J. Servon. 2007. "Reassessing the Role of Housing in Community-Based Urban Development." *Housing Policy Debate* 19 (4): 752–783.

Mohr, Holbrook. 2008. "Immigration Raid Called Nation's Biggest." *Boston Sunday Globe,* August 27.

Moskowitz, Eric. 2011. "Doubts Raised about Transit Project Funding." *Boston Sunday Globe,* October 30.

Mossberger, Karen, and Gerry Stoker. 2001. "The Evolution of Urban Regime Theory: The Challenge of Conceptualization." *Urban Affairs Review* 36, no. 6 (July): 810–835.

Mystic View Task Force (MVTF). 2006. "Final Settlement Agreement." Available at http://www.mysticview.org/docs/Final_Settlement_Agreement.pdf.

———. n.d. Mystic View Task Force History. Available at http://www.mysticview.org/mvtf_history.php.

Naples, Nancy, editor. 1998a. *Community Activism and Feminist Politics: Organizing across Race, Class, and Gender.* New York: Routledge.

———. 1998b. *Grassroots Warriors: Activist Mothering, Community Work, and the War on Poverty.* New York: Routledge.

Nash, Tom. 2008. "Somerville Immigrants Speak out against ICE Raids." *Somerville Journal,* August 13.

———. 2009a. "Transparency Fight Dominates BOA Meeting as Police Chief Defends Department." *Somerville News,* April 29.

———. 2009b. "Union Square Rezoning Plan Approved." *Somerville News,* April 29.

Newman, Janet, Marian Barnes, Helen Sullivan, and Andrew Knops. 2004. "Public Participation and Collaborative Governance." *Journal of Social Policy* 33 (April): 203–233.

Nguyen, Mai Thi. 2009. "Why Do Communities Mobilize against Growth: Growth Pressures, Community Status, Metropolitan Hierarchy, or Strategic Interaction?" *Journal of Urban Affairs* 31 (1): 25–43.

Nicas, Jack. 2008a. "Community Event Examines Immigration Raids," *Somerville News,* June 2.

———. 2008b. "Proposed T Stops Re-examined by Executive Office of Transportation." *Somerville News,* August 6.

Office of Housing and Community Development. 2002. *Union Square Transportation Plan.* Somerville, MA: City of Somerville.

Office of the Mayor. 2008. *2008 Resident Report.* Somerville, MA: City of Somerville.

Office of Strategic Planning and Community Development (OSPCD). 2008. *City of Somerville: Consolidated Plan 2008 to 2013.* Somerville, MA: City of Somerville.

———. 2009a. *Trends in Somerville: Economic Trends.* Somerville, MA: City of Somerville.

———. 2009b. *Trends in Somerville: Population Technical Report.* Somerville, MA: City of Somerville.

Ohlemacher, Stephen. 2008a. "Immigration Boom Slows as Economy Falters." *Boston Globe,* September 23.

———. 2008b. "Report: Illegal Immigration Falls." *Boston Globe,* October 3.

Okamoto, Dina, and Kim Ebert. 2010. "Beyond the Ballot: Immigrant Collective Action in Gateways and New Destinations." *Social Problems* 57 (4): 529–558.

Organisation for Economic Co-operation and Development. 2001. *Cities for Citizens: Improving Metropolitan Governance.* Paris: OECD.

Ostrander, Susan A. 1984. *Women of the Upper Class.* Philadelphia: Temple University Press.

————. 1999. "Gender and Race in a Pro-feminist, Progressive, Mixed-Gender, Mixed-Race Organization." *Gender and Society* 13, no. 5 (October): 609–627.

————. 2004a. "Democracy, Civic Participation, and the University: A Comparative Study of Civic Engagement on Five Campuses." *Nonprofit and Voluntary Sector Quarterly* 33 (1): 74–92.

————. 2004b. "Moderating Contradictions of Feminist Philanthropy: Women's Community Organizations and the Boston Women's Fund, 1995 to 2000." *Gender and Society* 18, no. 1 (February): 29–46.

————. 2012. "Agency and Initiative by Community Associations in Relations of Shared Governance: Between Civil Society and Local State." *Community Development Journal.* doi:10.1093/cdj/bss051. Advance access.

Ostrander, Susan A., and Kent E. Portney, editors. 2007. *Acting Civically: From Urban Neighborhoods to Higher Education.* Hanover, NH/Medford, MA: New England University Press/Tufts University Press.

Pantoja, Adrian D., Ricardo Ramirez, and Gary M. Segura. 2001. "Citizens by Choice, Voters by Necessity: Patterns in Political Mobilization by Naturalized Latinos." *Political Research Quarterly* 54, no. 4 (December): 729–750.

Parker, Brock. 2004. "Somerville, with $1M Homes?" *Somerville Journal*, March 25.

————. 2005a. "Dems Get More Progressive, Make Inroads in Somerville." *Somerville Journal*, February 10.

————. 2005b. "Immigration Crushes City's Ability to Help," *Somerville Journal*, July 14.

————. 2005c. "Teens Say 'Save Our Somerville,' Not Attack Yuppies." *Somerville Journal*, October 20.

Perez, Gina M. 2002. "The Other 'Real World': Gentrification and the Social Construction of Place in Chicago." *Urban Anthropology* 31, no. 1 (Spring): 37–68.

Portney, Kent E., and Jeffrey M. Berry. 1997. "Mobilizing Minority Communities: Social Capital and Participation in Urban Neighborhoods." *American Behavioral Scientist* 40, no. 5 (March/April): 632–644.

Powers, Kathleen, and Susan May Danseyar. 2001. "Can't Afford the Rent Hike?" *Somerville Journal*, July 16.

Preston, Julia. 2010a. "Deportations from U.S. Hit a Record High." *New York Times*, October 7.

————. 2010b. "Hispanics Cite Bias in Survey." *New York Times*, October 29.

————. 2010c. "Study Finds the Number of Illegal Immigrants Has Fallen to 11.1 Million." *New York Times*, September 2.

————. 2011. "Latinos and Democrats Press Obama to Curb Deportations." *New York Times*, April 21.

Preston, Julia, and Robert Gebeloff. 2010. "Unlicensed Drivers Who Risk More Than a Fine." *New York Times*, December 10.

Putnam, Robert, 1995. "Bowling Alone: America's Declining Social Capital." *Journal of Democracy* 6 (1): 65–78.

————. 2000. *Bowling Alone: The Collapse and Revival of American Community.* New York: Simon and Schuster.

Ramakrishnan, S. Karthick, and Irene Bloemraad. 2008a. "Introduction: Civic and Political Inequalities." In *Civic Hopes and Political Realities: Immigrants, Commu-*

nity Organizations, and Political Engagement, edited by S. Karthick Ramakrishnan and Irene Bloemraad, 1–42. New York: Russell Sage Foundation.

———. 2008b. "Making Organizations Count: Immigrant Civic Engagement in California Cities." In *Civic Hopes and Political Realities: Immigrants, Community Organizations, and Political Engagement*, edited by S. Karthick Ramakrishnan and Irene Bloemraad, 45–76. New York: Russell Sage Foundation.

Reidy, Chris. 2006. "IKEA Hopeful Its Somerville Project on Track." *Boston Globe*, August 15.

Rezendes, M. 2009. "Passionate Sense of Right and Wrong Drives Capuano." *Boston Globe*, November 16.

Ross, Casey. 2012. "Ikea Pulls Plan for Somerville Store in Assembly Square." Available at boston.com. July 20.

Sacchetti, Maria. 2008a. "Deportations in N.E. Increased from Last Year." *Boston Globe*, November 7.

———. 2008b. "Drive Aims to Boost Voting by Immigrants." *Boston Globe*, September 19.

———. 2008c. "Initiative Seeks to Aid Immigrants." *Boston Globe*, July 10.

———. 2008d. "Obama Faces Pressure on Immigration Reform." *Boston Globe*, November 17.

———. 2009a. "Agencies Halt Their Immigrant Scrutiny." *Boston Globe*, October 2.

———. 2009b. "Fees Deter Many from Citizenship." *Boston Globe*, September 20.

———. 2009c. "Immigrant Tax Impact Assessed in Report." *Boston Globe*, June 24.

———. 2009d. "Tuition, Driver's Licenses Urged for Illegal Immigrants." *Boston Globe*, November 17.

———. 2009e. "Widen Right to Drive, Say Chiefs," *Boston Globe*, April 20.

———. 2010a. "Illegal Immigrant Students Tell of Lost Opportunities." *Boston Globe*, November 26.

———. 2010b. "On Immigration, Patrick Is Measured." *Boston Globe*, July 22.

———. 2010c. "Patrick to Focus on Change for Immigrants." *Boston Globe*, November 17.

———. 2010d. "State Joins U.S. Push in Illegal Immigrants." *Boston Globe*, December 18.

Samburg, Bridget, 2003. "Somerville: Getting Citizenship, Tough and Tougher." *Boston Globe*, February 23.

Sampson, Robert J., Doug McAdam, Heather MacIndoe, and Simon Weffer-Elizondo. 2005. "Civil Society Reconsidered: The Durable Nature and Community Structure of Collective Civic Action," *American Journal of Sociology* 11, no. 3 (November): 673–714.

Shelton, William C. 2005. "What to Do about Gentrification?" *Somerville News*, November 18.

———. 2007. "Changing Population: Unchanging Political Culture." *Somerville News*, June 26.

Silverman, Robert Mark. 2005. "Caught in the Middle: Community Development Corporations (CDCs) and the Conflict between Grassroots and Instrumental Forms of Citizen Participation." *Community Development* 36 (2): 35–51.

Sirianni, Carmen. 2009. *Investing in Democracy: Engaging Citizens in Collaborative Governance*. Washington, DC: Brookings Institute.

Skocpol, Theda. 2003. *Diminished Democracy: From Membership to Management in American Civic Life*. Norman: University of Oklahoma Press.

Skocpol, Theda, and Morris R. Fiorina. 1999. "Making Sense of the Civic Engagement Debate." In *Civic Engagement in American Democracy*, edited by T. Skocpol and M. R. Fiorina, 1–24. New York: Russell Sage Foundation.

Smith, D. H., R. A. Stebbins, and M. A. Dover. 2006. *A Dictionary of Nonprofit Terms and Concepts*. Bloomington: Indiana University Press.

Smith, Erin. 2009a. "SHS Students Say Somerville Police Officer Hit Them, Falsely Accused Them of Being Gang Ringleaders." *Somerville News*, March 19.

———. 2009b. "Somerville Police Change Policy on Gangs after Teen's Story." *Somerville News*, April 29.

Smock, Kristina. 2004. *Democracy in Action: Community Organizing and Urban Change*. New York: Columbia University Press.

Sobieraj, Sarah, and Deborah White. 2007. "Could Civic Engagement Reproduce Political Inequality?" In *Acting Civically: From Urban Neighborhoods to Higher Education*, edited by Susan A. Ostrander and Kent E. Portney, 92–110. Hanover, NH/Medford, MA: New England University Press/Tufts University Press.

Somerville Community Corporation. n.d. Available at http://www.Somervillecdc.org/GetInvolved/joinacommittee.html. Accessed July 6, 2009.

Somerville Voices. n.d. Available at http://www.somervillevoices.org/2008/12/04/development-and-zoning. Accessed December 8, 2008.

Stolle, Dietlind, and Thomas R. Rochon. 1998. "Are All Associations Alike? Member Diversity, Asssociational Types, and the Creation of Social Capital." *American Behavioral Scientist* 42, no. 1 (September): 47–65.

Stone, Clarence. 1993. "Urban Regimes and the Capacity to Govern: A Political Economy Approach." *Journal of Urban Affairs* 15:1–28.

Strauss, Claudia. 2006. "The Imaginary." *Anthropological Theory* 6 (3): 322–344.

Strom, Elizabeth. 2008, "Rethinking the Politics of Downtown Development." *Journal of Urban Affairs* 30 (1): 37–61.

Sullivan, Daniel Moore. 2007. "Re-assessing Gentrification: Measuring Residents' Opinions Using Survey Data." *Urban Affairs Review* 42, no. 4 (March): 583–592.

Swidley, Neil. 2004. "Would You Pay a Million Dollars for This?" *Boston Globe*. September 12.

Taylor, Marilyn. 2007. "Community Participation in the Real World: Opportunities and Pitfalls in New Governance Spaces." *Urban Studies* 44, no. 2 (February): 297–317.

Theiss-Morse, Elizabeth, and John R. Hibbing. 2005. "Citizenship and Civic Engagement." *Annual Review of Political Science* 8:227–249.

Tooby, Norton, 2005. *Deportation Grounds Checklist*. Available at http://www.criminalandimmigrationlaw.com/~crimwcom/public/Deportation_Grounds_Checklist.pdf. Accessed January 2009.

"Too Little, Too Late." Editorial. 2011. *New York Times*, June 20.

Ueda, Reed. 1987. *Avenues to Adulthood: The Origins of the High School and Social Mobility in an American Suburb*. New York: Cambridge University Press.

U.S. Census Bureau. 1990. Age by Citizenship. American Fact Finder.

———. 2000a. Place of Birth by Citizenship Status. American Fact Finder.

————. 2000b. Profile of Selected Characteristics. American Fact Finder. Geographic Area: Somerville, Massachusetts.

————. 2005. Somerville, Massachusetts. Population and Housing Narrative Profile. American Community Survey.

————. 2007. Citizenship Statues in the United States. American Community Survey.

"Using Police on Immigration Is Only Justified for Criminals." Editorial. 2010. *Boston Globe*, December 21.

Van Der Heiden, Jeremy F. 2009. "Infrastructure and Transportation Trends Assessed." *Somerville News*, August 12.

Varsanyi, Monica W., editor. 2010. *Taking Local Control: Immigration Policy Activism in U.S. Cities and States*. Stanford, CA: Stanford University Press.

Verba, S., K. L. Schlozman, and H. E. Brady. 1995. *Voice and Equality: Civic Voluntarism in American Politics*. Cambridge, MA: Harvard University Press.

Walker, Edward T. 2008. "Contingent Pathways from Joiner to Activist: The Indirect Effects of Participation in Voluntary Associations on Civic Engagement." *Sociological Forum* 23, no. 1 (March): 116–143.

Walsh, Katherine Cramer, M. Kent Jennings, and Laura Stoker. 2004. "The Effects of Social Class Identification on Participatory Orientations towards Government." *British Journal of Political Science* 34, no. 3 (July): 469–496.

Wamunyu, Wambui. 1999. "Starbucks Reassures Residents." *Somerville Journal*, July 20.

Warren, Mark E. 2001. *Democracy and Association*. Princeton, NJ: Princeton University Press.

Warren, Mark R. 2001. *Dry Bones Rattling: Community Building to Revitalize American Democracy*. Princeton, NJ: Princeton University Press.

Waters, Mary C., and Reed Ueda, editors. 2007. "Introduction." *The New Americans: A Guide to Immigration since 1965*. Cambridge, MA: Harvard University Press.

Weir, Margaret. 2010. "Collaborative Government and Civic Empowerment." Book review of Carmen Sirianni's *Investing in Government*. *Perspectives on Politics* 8, no. 2 (June): 595–598.

Welcome Project. 2011. Mission Statement. Available at www.welcomeproject.org. Accessed January 13, 2013.

Wells, Miriam. J. 2004. "The Grassroots Reconfiguration of U.S. Immigration Policy." *International Migration Review* 38, no. 4 (Winter): 1308–1347.

White, Stephen, Neil Nevitte, Andre Blais, Elizabeth Gidengil, and Patrick Fournier. 2008. "The Political Re-socialization of Immigrants: Resistance or Lifelong Learning." *Political Research Quarterly* 61:268–281.

Wright, Erick Olin. 1997. *Class Counts: Comparative Studies in Class Analysis*. Cambridge: Cambridge University Press.

Wuthnow, Robert. 1991. "The Voluntary Sector: Legacy of the Past, Hope for the Future?" In *Between States and Markets: The Voluntary Sector in Comparative Perspective*, edited by Robert Wuthnow, 3–29. Princeton, NJ: Princeton University Press.

————. 1998. *Loose Connections: Joining Together in America's Fragmented Communities*. Princeton, NJ: Princeton University Press.

———. 2002. "The United States: Bridging the Privileged and the Marginalized?" In *Democracies in Flux: The Evolution of Social Capital in Contemporary Society*, edited by R. Putnam, 59–102. New York: Oxford University Press.

Yen, Hope. 2009. "Hispanic, Asian Growth Slowing, Census Says." *Boston Globe*, May 14.

Zukin, Sharon. 2009. "New Retail Capital and Neighborhood Change: Boutiques and Gentrification." *City and Community* 8, no. 1 (March): 47–64.

Index

Susan A. Ostrander is Professor of Sociology, School of Arts and Sciences, and Professor, Jonathan M. Tisch College of Citizenship and Public Service, at Tufts University. She is the author of *Money for Change: Social Movement Philanthropy at Haymarket People's Fund* and *Women of the Upper Class* (both Temple).